C000047012

"*The Rule of Faith* is an ⟨
the ancient church, and
to its early history and development
collection of the most relevant primary texts and expert analysis
by one of our most distinguished scholars of Christian origins
. . . A splendid achievement!"

—DAVID G. HUNTER, Cottrill-Rolfes Chair of Catholic Studies,
University of Kentucky

THE RULE OF FAITH

Cascade Companions

The Christian theological tradition provides an embarrassment of riches: from Scripture to modern scholarship, we are blessed with a vast and complex theological inheritance. And yet this feast of traditional riches is too frequently inaccessible to the general reader.

The Cascade Companions series addresses the challenge by publishing books that combine academic rigor with broad appeal and readability. They aim to introduce nonspecialist readers to that vital storehouse of authors, documents, themes, histories, arguments, and movements that comprise this heritage with brief yet compelling volumes.

TITLES IN THIS SERIES:

Reading Paul by Michael J. Gorman

Theology and Culture by D. Stephen Long

Creationism and the Conflict over Evolution by Tatha Wiley

Justpeace Ethics by Jarem T. Sawatsky

Reading Bonhoeffer by Geffrey B. Kelly

Christianity and Politics in America by C. C. Pecknold

Philippians in Context by Joseph H. Hellerman

Reading Revelation Responsibly by Michael J. Gorman

The Rule of Faith

A Guide

Everett Ferguson

CASCADE *Books* · Eugene, Oregon

THE RULE OF FAITH
A Guide

Cascade Companions 20

Cascade Books
A Division of Wipf and Stock Publishers
199 W. 8th Ave., Suite 3
Eugene, OR 97401

www.wipfandstock.com

ISBN 13: 978-1-62564-759-7

Cataloging-in-Publication data:

Ferguson, Everett, 1933–.

The rule of faith : a guide / Everett Ferguson.

xii + 104 p. ; 20.5 cm. Includes bibliographical references and index.

Cascade Companions 20

ISBN 13: 978-1-62564-759-7

1. Theology, Doctrinal—History—Early church, ca. 30–600. 2. Church history—Primitive and early church, ca. 30–600. 3. Fathers of the church. 4. Creeds. I. Series. II. Title.

BR195.C5 F47 2015

To my students—
  Past (in classes I taught)
  Present (through my writings)
  Future (as the Lord wills)—
    May they take truth, faith, and piety as
    their rules of life

Contents

Preface xi

ONE: Statements of the Rule of Faith/Canon of
Truth 1

TWO: Notes on Terminology and Other Pertinent
Statements 16

THREE: Interpretation of the Rule of Faith 34

FOUR: Studies of the Rule of Faith 48

FIVE: Functions of the Rule of Faith 67

SIX: Relevance for Today of the Rule of Faith 83

Bibliography 91

Indexes

Preface

Early Christian writers frequently spoke of what has come to be termed the rule of faith under various terms, such as "canon of truth," "rule of piety," "ecclesiastical rule," in addition to "rule of faith." The summaries of Christian doctrine so designated flourished in the second and third centuries. With the fourth and fifth centuries the general agreement on a canon of Scripture and adoption of ecumenical creeds gave a different flavor to the terminology of "rule of faith."

Part of the concern in this book is to clarify the relation of the rule of faith to Scripture and creed. Briefly put, my thesis is that the rule of faith was a summary of apostolic preaching and teaching, to be found most authoritatively in written form in the Scriptures. Although often identified with the baptismal confession of faith and thus with creeds, the rule was distinct and had a different function. The overlap in contents between what was taught and what was confessed led to a blurring of this distinction and has caused confusion because many studies have covered the rule of faith only as related to the history of creeds or even identified the rule of faith with a creed.

There has been no shortage of studies of the rule of faith in the early church, as the survey of scholarship in chapter four demonstrates. There does not seem to be, however, a recent comprehensive study that brings together evidence from the ancient sources with an interpretation of the meaning and functions of the rule of faith. This little book attempts such a comprehensive overview and concludes with a few words on the relevance of the rule of faith for churches today.

Biblical quotations are from the New Revised Standard Version. Translations from non-biblical writings, unless otherwise credited, are my own, but in some cases are only slightly modified from older translations.

ONE

Statements of the Rule of Faith/Canon of Truth

What is it that Christians are to believe and proclaim? How do we know whether a certain belief falls within or without the boundaries of a Christian faith that seeks to be true to its ancient origins? When is our message authentically Christian? Many today are suspicious of those who try to tell us what we have to believe, and feel that notions of orthodoxy and heresy are oppressive and unhelpful: that individual Christians can decide for themselves what counts as Christian. What do Christians believe? For many the answer to this question is "whatever it is that people who choose to self-identify as Christians claim to believe." So belief in the Trinity is Christian, but *so is its denial;* belief in the deity of Christ is Christian, *but so is its rejection;* belief in the resurrection is Christian, *but so is disbelief.* The problem with such an approach is that pretty much any belief can have a claim to being authentically Christian, and when a label becomes that elastic, it loses any hope of meaning anything.

The early Jesus communities were diverse groupings and there were disputes and tussles within them as to what belief constituted legitimate parts of the Christian proclamation. But from very early on there was a widely shared consensus—at least within those Jesus communities that saw themselves as directly linked to the ministry of the apostles—as to the basic shape of the church's proclamation. There was still plenty of scope for disagreement and development, but the sense of the core of "the faith once for all delivered to the saints" (Jude 3) was shared in common. And this core, this heart, was summed up in the rule of faith.

In order adequately to make sense of the church's rule of faith—what it was, how it functioned, and why it mattered so much—I will need to present a lot of raw data. Without at least a basic familiarity with this data it is hard to speak intelligently of the rule. So the first two chapters will major on presenting the key texts and terminology. This may be a little overwhelming, but bear with me. My hope is that by the end of the book you will see that all the complex data can be made sense of by a rather simple hypothesis. And my hope is that once this is all clarified in chapter 5, you will appreciate just how important the rule of faith was and why it remains so for the church today.

We begin by considering the classic presentations of the rule of faith. The terminology used was fluid, and different early Christian authors spoke variously of the "rule of faith," "the faith," the "canon of truth," "truth," or similar expressions. By these terms they referred to *summaries of the faith preached and taught by the churches.*

Justin Martyr

I begin with an early summary of Christian faith that does not use the terminology related to a rule of faith but that includes some of the items customarily found under this heading. It occurs at the beginning of the examination of the Christian teacher Justin Martyr by the Roman prefect Rusticus about 165. In answer to the question of Rusticus, "What is your dogma?" Justin replied:

> We piously believe in the God of the Christians, whom we regard to be the only one of these things from the beginning, the Maker and Fashioner of the whole creation, what is visible and invisible; and the Lord Jesus Christ, Child of God, who was proclaimed beforehand by the prophets as one who was going to be present with the race of humanity, the herald of salvation and teacher of good doctrines.
>
> (*Acts of Justin* 2, recension B)

Irenaeus

Irenaeus, writing in the180s and 190s, gave the earliest full listings of the main items. Irenaeus was the bishop of Lyons from about 178 to 202. Troubled by the teachings of various thinkers now commonly designated as "Gnostics," he produced his major work, "Five Books of Unmasking and Overthrow of the Gnosis Falsely So-Called," usually cited as *Against Heresies* (*Adversus Haereses*). We quote three statements from this work of the "immoveable truth proclaimed by the church" (*Against Heresies* 1.9.5) in contrast to the differing teachings offered by Gnostics. Another work, *Demonstration of the Apostolic Preaching,* a guide of the teaching to be given to new converts, provides a comparable summary.

> For the church, although dispersed throughout the whole world, as far as the ends of the earth, received from the apostles and their disciples, the faith in one God the Father Almighty, who has made the heaven, the earth, the seas, and all things in them; and in one Christ Jesus the Son of God, who was made flesh for our salvation; and in the Holy Spirit, who has proclaimed through the prophets the plans of God and the comings of Christ, both the birth from the virgin, the passion, the rising from the dead, and the bodily ascension into heaven of the beloved Christ Jesus our Lord, and his coming [again] from heaven in the glory of the Father for the summing up of all things and the raising of all humanity, in order that to Christ Jesus, our Lord, God, Savior, and King, according to the good pleasure of the invisible Father, "every knee should bow, of things in heaven, in earth, and under the earth, and that every tongue should confess" to him [Phil 2:10–11], and that he might make a just judgment on all, that he might send the spiritual hosts of wickedness, the angels who transgressed and went into apostasy, and the impious, unjust, lawless, and blasphemers among human beings into the eternal fire; but might grant incorruptible life and eternal glory to those who are righteous, holy, and keep his commandments, and who persevere in his love either from the beginning or by repentance, and surround them with eternal glory.
>
> (*Against Heresies* 1.10.1)

> Many nations of those barbarians who believe in Christ give their assent, . . . believing in one

God, Creator of heaven and earth and all things in them, through Christ Jesus the Son of God. He because of his preeminent love for his creation submitted to birth from a virgin, uniting through himself man to God, and having suffered under Pontius Pilate, and rising again, and being received in splendor, coming [again] in glory, the Savior of those who are saved and Judge of those who are judged, sending into eternal fire those who change the truth.

(*Against Heresies* 3.4.2)

He has a full faith in one God Almighty, from whom are all things; and a firm persuasion concerning the Son of God, Christ Jesus our Lord, by whom are all things, and his arrangements by which the Son of God became a man; and in the Spirit of God, who produces a recognition of the truth, who sets forth the arrangements of the Father and the Son to dwell among human beings in each generation, even as the Father wills.

(*Against Heresies* 4.33.7)

And this is the drawing up of our faith, the foundation of the building, and the consolidation of a way of life. God, the Father, uncreated, beyond grasp, invisible, one God the maker of all; this is the first and foremost article of our faith. But the second article is the Word of God, the Son of God, Christ Jesus our Lord, who was shown forth by the prophets according to the design of their prophecy and according to the manner in which the Father disposed, and through Him were made all things whatsoever. He also, in the end of times, for the recapitulation of all things, is become a man among men, visible and tangible, in order to abolish death and bring to

> light life, and bring about the communion of
> God and man. And the third article is the Holy
> Spirit, through whom the prophets prophesied
> and the patriarchs were taught about God and
> the just were led in the path of justice, and who
> in the end of times has been poured forth in a
> new manner upon humanity over all the earth
> renewing man to God.[1]
>
> (*Demonstration of the Apostolic Preaching* 6)

Tertullian

Tertullian of Carthage was the first prolific Christian writer
in Latin. His writings—which cover apologetic, anti-heretical, and moral/disciplinary subjects—come from about 196
to 212. He gives three statements of the rule of faith.[2]

> The rule of faith which is believed: there is but
> one God, and he alone is the creator of the
> world, who by the sending forth of his Word in
> the beginning brought the universe into being
> out of nothing; and this Word, called his Son,
> was seen in various ways in the name of God by
> the patriarchs, was heard always in the prophets,
> and last of all was brought down into the virgin
> Mary by the Spirit and power of God the Father,
> was made flesh in her womb and was born from
> her as Jesus Christ; thereafter he proclaimed
> a new law and a new promise of the kingdom
> of heaven, worked miracles, was nailed to the
> cross, was resurrected on the third day, was tak-
> en up to heaven to sit at the Father's right hand

1. Translation by Joseph P. Smith, *St. Irenaeus Proof of the Apostolic Preaching*, 51.

2. L. W. Countryman, "Tertullian and the *Regula Fidei*," gives the
Latin texts of the three versions in parallel columns.

and to send in his place the power of the Holy Spirit to guide believers, and will come again in glory to take the saints into the enjoyment of life eternal and heavenly promises, and to condemn the impious to everlasting fire, both parties being raised from the dead and having their flesh restored.

(*On the Prescription of Heretics* 13)

The rule of faith is entirely one, alone immoveable and unchangeable. The rule is that of believing in the one almighty God, the Founder of the universe, and in his Son Jesus Christ, born from the virgin Mary, crucified under Pontius Pilate, raised from the dead on the third day, received into the heavens, sitting now at the right [hand] of the Father, going to come to judge the living and the dead through the resurrection of the flesh. . . . This law of faith is constant.

(*On the Veiling of Virgins* 1.3–4)

We believe in one only God, nevertheless under this dispensation (which we call "economy") that there is a Son of the one God, his very Word which proceeds from him, through whom all things were made and without whom nothing has been made [John 1:1–3]. This one was sent by the Father into the virgin and from her was born man and God, Son of Man and Son of God, named Jesus Christ. This One suffered, this One died and was buried according to the Scriptures [1 Cor 15:3–4], was raised by the Father and taken back into heaven to sit at the right [hand] of the Father, will come to judge the living and the dead. He furthermore, according to his promise [John 16:7], sent from the Father the Holy Spirit, the Paraclete, the sanctifier of the

> faith of those who believe in the Father and Son
> and Holy Spirit. This rule has come down from
> the beginning of the gospel.

> (*Against Praxeas* 2)

Hippolytus

The writings of Hippolytus provide several difficulties.
More than one person bore this name, some works by
others may have been attributed to Hippolytus of Rome,
and which writings are to be ascribed to whom remains a
controversial matter. The author of a treatise *Against Noetus*
(*Contra haeresin Noeti*) may have been a presbyter named
Hippolytus in Rome in the first third of the third century.
He quotes against Noetus what the elders of the church of
Smyrna, apparently Noetus's home city, said they had been
taught.

> The presbyters replied to Noetus: "We too know
> in truth one God; we know Christ; we know that
> the Son suffered even as he suffered, and died
> even as he died, and rose again on the third
> day, and is at the right hand of the Father, and
> is coming to judge the living and the dead. And
> these things that we have learned we affirm."

> (*Against Noetus* 1)

Later in the treatise he summarizes his own understanding
of the scriptural testimonies.

> Let us believe then, blessed brothers, according
> to the tradition of the apostles, that God the
> Word came down from heaven into the holy vir-
> gin Mary in order that, taking flesh from her and
> assuming a human (by which I mean a rational)
> soul and thus becoming all that a human being

is, except for sin, he might save fallen humanity and confer immortality on those who believe on his name. In all, therefore, the word of truth is demonstrated to us, namely that the Father is One, whose Word also exists by whom he made all things, whom also, as we have said, the Father sent forth in latter times for the salvation of human beings. This one was preached by the Law and the Prophets as appointed to come into the world. And even as he was preached formerly, in the same manner also did he come and manifest himself, being by the virgin and the Holy Spirit made a new man; for having the heavenly from the Father as his Word and the earthly by taking to himself the flesh from the old Adam by means of the virgin, he now coming into the world was manifested as God in a body, coming forth as a perfect man. For it was not according to mere appearance or changeableness, but in truth that he became man.

Thus then, though demonstrated as God, he did not refuse the conditions proper to him as a human being. . . . [There follows an eloquent summary of the paradoxes of Christ's divine nature in the midst of his human life. The author then concludes:] This one breathes upon the disciples, gives them the Spirit, and comes among them when the doors are shut, and is taken up by a cloud into the heavens while the disciples look at him, is set down on the right hand of the Father, and comes again as the Judge of the living and the dead. This is the God who for our sakes became a human being, to whom also the Father has put all things in subjection. To him be the glory and the power, with the Father and the Holy Spirit, in the holy church both now and forever. Amen.

(*Against Noetus* 17–18)

Didascalia Apostolorum

The "Teaching of the Apostles" (*Didascalia Apostolorum*) is a manual of church order from the first half of the third century. It survives in Syriac and was incorporated with modifications in the fourth-century Greek *Apostolic Constitutions*. I translate the conclusion of the document from the Latin version.

> Therefore to him who is able to open the ears of your heart so that you may receive the words of the Lord which are provided through the gospel and doctrine of Jesus Christ the Nazarene, who was crucified under Pontius Pilate and slept so that he might evangelize Abraham, Isaac, Jacob, and all his saints concerning both the end of the age and the coming resurrection of the dead; and he was raised from the dead so that he might demonstrate and give to us a guarantee of the resurrection; and he was taken up into heaven through the power of God and his Spirit, and seated at the right hand of the throne of the Almighty God above the cherubim; who is coming with excellence and glory to judge the living and the dead. To him is the power, glory, majesty, and dominion, to the Father and the Son, who was and is and will be, both now and in all generations and in the ages of the ages. Amen.

Origen

Origen (ca. 185–ca. 251) was the most learned and prolific Greek author of the early church. He was a teacher in Alexandria and then in Caesarea in Palestine. In his *On First Principles* (*De principiis*) in the preface he set forth the undisputed Christian doctrines in distinction from those topics lacking clarity and about which one could speculate. Since the Greek does not survive, I quote the statements of the essential teachings, preserved in the Latin translation of Rufinus.

> The holy apostles, when preaching the faith of Christ, took certain doctrines, those namely which they believed to be necessary ones, and delivered them in the plainest terms to all believers. . . .
>
> The kind of doctrines which are believed in plain terms through the apostolic teaching are the following:—
>
> First, that God is one, who created and set in order all things, and who, when nothing existed, caused the universe to be. He is God from the first creation and foundation of the world, the God of all righteous men, of Adam, Abel, Seth, Enos, Enoch, Noah, Shem, Abraham, Isaac, Jacob, and the twelve patriarchs, of Moses and the prophets. This God, in these last days, according to the previous announcements made through his prophets, sent the Lord Jesus Christ, first for the purpose of calling Israel, and secondly, after the unbelief of the people of Israel, of calling the Gentiles also. This just and good God, the Father of our Lord Jesus Christ, himself gave the Law, the Prophets, and the Gospels, and he is God both of the apostles and also of the Old and New Testaments.
>
> Then again: Christ Jesus, he who came to earth, was begotten of the Father before every created thing [Jerome says that Origen wrote, "not begotten"]. And after he had ministered to the Father in the foundation of all things, "for all things were made through him" [John 1:3], in these last times he emptied himself and was made man, was made flesh, although he was

God; and being made man, he still remained what he was, namely, God. He took to himself a body like our body, differing in this alone, that it was born of a virgin and the Holy Spirit. And this Jesus Christ was born and suffered in truth and not merely in appearance, and truly died our common death. Moreover he truly rose from the dead, and after the resurrection associated with his disciples and was then taken up into heaven.

Then again, the apostles delivered this doctrine, that the Holy Spirit is united in honor and dignity with the Father and the Son. . . . It is, however, certainly taught with the utmost clearness in the church, that this Spirit inspired each one of the saints, both the prophets and the apostles, and that there was not one Spirit in the men of old and another in those who were inspired at the coming of Christ.

Next after this the apostles taught that the soul, having a substance and life of its own, will be rewarded according to its deserts after its departure from this world; for it will either obtain an inheritance of eternal life and blessedness, if its deeds shall warrant this, or it must be given over to eternal fire and torments, if the guilt of its crimes shall so determine. Further, there will be a time for the resurrection of the dead, when this body, which is now "sown in corruption" shall "rise in incorruption," and that which is "sown in dishonor" shall "rise in glory" [1 Cor 15:42–43].

This also is laid down in the church's teaching, that every rational soul is possessed of free will and choice; and also, that it is engaged in a struggle against the devil and his angels and the opposing powers; for these strive to weigh the soul down with sins, whereas we, if we lead a wise and upright life, endeavor to free ourselves from such a burden. There follows from this the conviction that we are not subject to necessity, so as to be compelled by every means, even against our will, to do either good or evil. . . .

Further, in regard to the devil and his angels and the opposing spiritual powers, the church teaching lays it down that these beings exist, but what they are or how they exist it has not explained very clearly. . . .

The church teaching also includes the doctrine that this world was made and began to exist at a definite time and that by reason of its corruptible nature it must suffer dissolution. . . .

Then there is the doctrine that the Scriptures were composed through the Spirit of God and that they have not only that meaning which is obvious, but also another which is hidden from the majority of readers. For the contents of Scripture are the outward forms of certain mysteries and images of divine things.[3]

(*On First Principles*, preface 3–8)

Novatian

Novatian was a presbyter in the church of Rome (mid-third century) who then went into schism and became a counter-bishop in Rome. He is the first major author in Rome to write in Latin. His treatise *On the Trinity* is an important theological contribution.

> The rule of truth requires that we believe, first of all, in God the Father and Lord Almighty, that is, the absolutely perfect Creator of all things.
>
> (*On the Trinity* 1)

3. The translation with some slight modifications is by G. W. Butterworth, *Origen on First Principles*, 2–5.

The same rule of truth teaches us to believe after the Father also in the Son of God, Christ Jesus, the Lord our God, but the Son of God. We are to believe in this Son of this God, who is both the one and the only God, namely the Creator of all things. . . . This Jesus Christ, I repeat, the Son of this God, we read was not only promised in the Old Testament but we observe also to have been manifested in the New Testament, fulfilling the shadows and figures of all the mysteries, in his presence the embodiment of truth. [There follow prophecies of his virgin birth, miracles, humility, passion, resurrection, the faith of Gentiles and unbelief of Jews, his session at God's right hand, and coming judgment.]

(*On the Trinity* 9)

Moreover, the order of reason and the authority of the faith . . . admonish us to believe after these things [concerning the Father and the Son] also in the Holy Spirit, who was formerly promised to the church and given in the appointed, proper time. For he was promised by the prophet Joel [Joel 3:2] and given by Christ. . . . Therefore, there is one and the same Spirit who was in the prophets and in the apostles, except that in the former he was occasional but in the latter always. . . . This is he who orders the rule of truth . . . [and] guards the gospel.

(*On the Trinity* 29)

Victorinus of Pettau

Victorinus lived in the second half of the third century and was bishop of Petovium in what is now Slovenia.

The command of God is to confess the Father Almighty, that his Son Christ was begotten by the Father before the beginning of the world and was made man in true soul and flesh, . . . and that when he was received with his body into heaven by the Father, he gave forth the Holy Spirit, the gift and pledge of immortality, that he was announced by the Prophets, was described by the Law, was God's hand and the Word of the Father from God, Lord over all and founder of the world. This is the canon and measure of faith, and no one worships at the holy altar except the one who confesses this faith (11.1).

(*Commentary on the Apocalypse*)

Discussion Questions

1. Which statement of the Rule of Faith do you find most adequate? Why?

2. What items do most of the statements of the Rule of Faith have in common?

3. Do you find these statements to be in harmony with the Bible? Are any items included in the Rule of Faith not in harmony with the Bible?

4. Does the preaching/teaching in your church reflect the contents found in the Rule of Faith?

TWO

Notes on Terminology
and Other Pertinent Statements

There are numerous references in early Christian literature to a rule as a standard of belief and practice without spelling out the content of this rule. These passages commonly used the Greek word *kanōn* (κανών), which meant a rule or a standard, or the Latin *regula*, which had the same meanings.

First Clement provides an early example of the general usage out of which the later writers developed a semi-technical terminology. This letter of the church at Rome to the church at Corinth refers to the "rule of obedience" directed by wives to their husbands (1.3) and the "appointed rule of his ministry" that a presbyter was not to go beyond (41.1). Particularly relevant to later developments is the exhortation, "Let us leave behind empty and vain thoughts and come to the well esteemed and noble rule of our tradition" (7.2). The Greek word for rule in each case is *kanōn*.

Perhaps the first to use the phrase "canon of the truth" was Dionysius, bishop of Corinth (about 170). Eusebius reports that he wrote a letter to the church of Nicomedia, "in which he combats the heresy of Marcion and compares it to the rule of the truth" (*Church History* 4.23.4). This is an early example of a rule invoked for anti-heretical purposes.

A few years later Polycrates, bishop of Ephesus, in a letter to Victor, bishop of Rome, defending the date on which Christians in Asia observed the Pascha (Easter), used the phrase "canon of faith" (*kanona tēs pisteōs*—perhaps the first to use this phrase) as equivalent to "according to the gospel" (quoted by Eusebius, *Church History* 5.24.6). Not long after, in the early 200s, an anonymous author quoted by Eusebius referred to those who corrupted the word of God and "treated with contempt the rule of the ancient faith" (*pisteōs archaias kanona—Church History* 5.2813).

Irenaeus

The most extensive use of this language is found in Irenaeus, who wrote in Greek, but whose complete text is preserved only in an early Latin translation. Irenaeus's preferred term is "canon of truth" (*kanōn tēs alētheias, regula veritatis*). He appears to have derived this term and its basic idea from Philo of Alexandria, the Hellenistic Jewish philosopher.[1] By this phrase, Irenaeus meant not a standard for determining the truth *but truth itself as the standard.*[2] He states expressly, "Having then as a rule the truth itself" (*Against Heresies*

---

1. See Lanne, "La Règle de la Vérité," for the dependence of Irenaeus on Philo for this phrase. It refers in Irenaeus, he concludes, not to the symbol of faith, nor the letter of Scripture, nor tradition, but the whole of what the believer perceives of the mysteries that God himself reveals in its coherence (ibid., 70).

2. Ammundsen, "The Rule of Truth in Irenaeus." This meaning is pushed by Hägglund, "Die Bedeutung der 'regula fidei' als Grundlage theologischer Aussagen" (4–18 on Irenaeus).

2.28.1). This meaning is further evident in his usage. "We hold indeed to the rule of truth, that is, that there is one God Almighty, who established all things through his Word and formed and made all things out of that which was not so that they might exist" (*Against Heresies* 1.22.1); similarly, "The disciple of the Lord [i.e., the Apostle John], therefore, wishing to exclude all such ideas [those of Cerinthus and the Nicolaitans] and to establish the rule of truth in the church, that there is one God Almighty, who through his Word made all things, visible and invisible, . . ." followed by a quotation of John 1:1–5 (*Against Heresies* 3.11.1). Irenaeus refers to the person "who retains immovable in his heart the rule of truth received through baptism" (*Against Heresies* 1.9.4), probably referring to the instruction given in preparation for baptism. In one passage, Irenaeus uses "rule of truth," "truth," and "body of truth" for the things "set forth expressly without ambiguity in the holy Scriptures" (*Against Heresies* 2.27.1; cf. 3.12.6 for "truth" and "rule of truth" as interchangeable). Particularly clear is the following declaration: "For we follow our teacher, the one and only true God, and have his words as the rule of truth" (ibid. 4.35.4). The "rule of truth" is "the doctrine of the apostles" (*Against Heresies* 3.15.1). He could write just of "truth," as in the statement that "Justly therefore it is proved by us that [the heretics] diverged exceedingly far from the truth" (*Against Heresies* 2.30.9). He concluded his *Demonstration of the Apostolic Preaching* by saying that "This, beloved, is the preaching of the truth, and this is the manner of our salvation, and this is the way of life, announced by the prophets and ratified by Christ and handed over by the apostles and handed down by the church in the whole world to her children" (98).[3]

3. The work is preserved only in Armenian; translation by Joseph P. Smith, *St. Irenaeus Proof of the Apostolic Preaching*, 49.

Irenaeus once used "rule of faith," according to the Armenian translation of his *Demonstration of the Apostolic Preaching 6:* "We must keep strictly, without deviation, the rule of faith, and carry out the commands of God, believing in God and fearing him," and this "faith is given by truth, since faith rests upon reality."[4]

Clement of Alexandria

Clement of Alexandria had a varied terminology. *Kanōn* (canon or rule) is frequent in the general sense of criterion or rule for one's conduct (as in *Miscellanies* 4.15.98).[5] Thus he writes of the "rule" that one chooses in regard to celibacy (*Miscellanies* 3.12.79.4) and affirms that celibacy may be chosen "according to sound rule," if not from heretical asceticism (*Miscellanies* 3.18.105.1). Clement refused to surrender the word "gnostic" to the heretics and used it in an orthodox sense for truly knowing reality and living the Christian life. "Gentleness, kind-heartedness, and magnificent godliness are, I think, the rules of assimilation to the gnostic life" (*Miscellanies* 7.3.13.4).

Like Irenaeus, Clement used "canon of truth," but unlike him did not spell out its contents. He referred to the "gnostic tradition [concerning the natural world] according to the rule of truth" (*Miscellanies* 4.1.3.2). Again, like Irenaeus, by "canon of truth" Clement meant *truth itself* as the rule. Lovers of truth, "receiving the rule of truth from truth itself, possess the truth" (*Miscellanies* 7.16.94.5; cf. 7.16.105 for paralleling truth and the canon of the church). The body of truth learned from the Scriptures served in turn as a guide to interpreting the Scriptures: "explaining

4. Ibid., 108.
5. Van den Eynde, *Les Normes de l'Enseignement Chrétien*, 299.

the Scriptures according to the canon of truth" (*Miscellanies* 6.15.124.5).

A characteristic phrase for Clement was "rule of the church." Sometimes he words it "ecclesiastical rule" and sometimes "rule of the church." "We are showing that the only truly holy and godly person is the one really a gnostic according to the ecclesiastical rule [*ekklēsiastikon kanona/* ἐκκλησιαστικόν κανόνα]" (*Miscellanies* 7.7.41). Truth was the "ecclesiastical rule," and in discussing the truth, Clement stated, "It is proper for us in no way to transgress the ecclesiastical rule" (*Miscellanies* 7.15.90.5). The canon of the church was closely related to the Scriptures as well as to the truth. At the conclusion of a chapter making frequent reference to the Scriptures, Clement paralleled the truth and the rule of the church, applying both to conduct: "We must not be like those who follow the heresies to adulterate the truth and steal the rule of the church [*kanona tēs ekklēsias/* κανόνα τῆς ἐκκλησίας], by gratifying our own lusts and vanities" (*Miscellanies* 7.16.105.5). According to Clement, Paul "teaches knowledge, which is the completion of faith, those things that go beyond catechetical instruction according to the magnificence of the teaching of the Lord and the ecclesiastical rule" (*Miscellanies* 6.18.165). The rule of the church included matters of worship. Heresies that used bread and water instead of bread and wine in the eucharistic offering do so "not according to the rule of the church" (*Miscellanies* 1.19.96). The most explicit statement of content of the ecclesiastical rule is this important statement of the orthodox interpretation of Scripture: "Those who receive and preserve according to the ecclesiastical rule the interpretation of the Scriptures made clear by him; the rule of the church is the agreement and harmony of both the Law and the Prophets with the covenant delivered at the coming of the Lord" (*Miscellanies* 6.15.125.3). So common was this usage in Clement that Eusebius reports that Clement wrote a book now lost on "The Ecclesiastical Canon" (*Church History* 6.13.3).

Many of these passages are contrasting what distinguishes the faithful from heretics, but Clement has way of life as well as doctrine in mind in his usage of the rule. In a passage discussing celibate or married life, Clement, alluding to Galatians 2:14 and 6:16, speaks of "walking according to the truth in the evangelical rule" (*Miscellanies* 3.9.66).

Once Clement refers to the "famous and revered rule of tradition from the origin of the world" (*Miscellanies* 1.1.15.2). In the same chapter he appeals to the "tradition of the blessed teaching from the apostles."

In elaborating on his use of the word "gnostic," Clement speaks of "the gnostic rule." "Knowledge of the Son and the Father according to the gnostic rule, that is, what is truly gnostic, is the apprehension and comprehension of the truth through the truth" (*Miscellanies* 5.1.1.4). So, Clement brings us back to the association of the rule with truth.

Although Clement has passages referring to the principal Christian doctrines that other authors include in the rule of faith (e.g., *Miscellanies* 6.15.123 and 127—one God and Christ's incarnation in womb of the virgin, suffering, and rising again), he does not equate the rule with particular doctrines. Nor does he identify the rule with a confession of faith, in spite of stating that "we keep our confession of the most important points," in contrast to heretics (*Miscellanies* 7.15.90, following the statement quoted above).

Tertullian

Tertullian made frequent use of the word "rule" (*regula*), employing it in the sense of "norm" ("What is earlier provides the rule for what is later"—*Against Marcion* 1.9; cf.

5.19), "principle" ("This rule is required by the nature of the one and only God"—*Against Hermogenes* 17), "prescription" or "requirement" ("they agree with the rules, dispensations, and instructions of the Creator"—*Against Marcion* 5.8), and referring to the doctrines of a philosophical school ("the rules of philosophy"—*Against Marcion* 5.19) or of a heretical sect ("a faith which holds to a different rule"—*On the Flesh of Christ* 6; "swerve from their own rules"—*Prescription against Heretics* 42.7). But above all he uses rule for Christian doctrine.[6]

Tertullian, if not reflecting current usage, established "rule of faith" (*regula fidei*) as standard terminology in Latin and for the later Western church. He used the phrase for the definite content of Christian doctrine or more often for doctrine itself. Hence, when he used the genitives "of faith" or "of truth," these were genitives of apposition or possession, identifying the rule with faith or truth, and not referring to a standard for judging faith or truth.[7]

Aside from his use of "rule" for items other than the Christian faith ("everything is open to suspicion which is deprived of a rule"—*Against Marcion* 3.2.1), Tertullian had related terminology to the "rule of faith." For instance,

- Christian wisdom guides inquiry according to "the rules of God" (*On the Soul* 1.6);

- Marcion's conduct is to be investigated according to "the rule of Scripture" (*Against Marcion* 3.17.5), identifying Scripture as the rule;

- "rule of the mystery [*sacramenti*]" is that there is no other God than the Creator (*Against Marcion* 1.21.4; cf. 5.20 and "rights which no other rule directs than the one tradition of the selfsame mystery"—*Prescription*

---

6. Van den Eynde, *Les Normes*, 291–92.

7. Van den Eynde, *Les Normes*, 293.

Against Heretics 20.9);

- "the rule of truth" comes from Christ and was transmitted through his companions (*Apology* 47.10; cf. "the more ancient rule of truth"—*Against Hermogenes* 1, and rule associated with truth in *Against Marcion* 5.20);

- "rule of faith or hope" (*On Fasting* 1);

- "the rule" without other qualification: "The rule which has been always established previously gives its prescription against what comes later" (*Against Praxeas* 20.3), or in allusion to Galatians 6:16, "we walk by that rule which the church has received from the apostles, the apostles from Christ, and Christ from God" (*Prescription against Heretics* 37.1). The four Gospels all have as their premise the same rules (*Against Marcion* 4.2). Consequently, Tertullian had no patience with "arguments contrary . . . to our [catholic Christians'] rule" (*On the Soul* 2.7).

When "rule" is qualified in some way, "rule of faith" is Tertullian's preferred designation, as in the quotations in chapter 1. Even Marcion's teaching is designated as "our adversary's rule of faith" (*Against Marcion* 1.1.5). Marcion's followers claimed that he did not innovate on the rule by separating Law and Gospel, but restored it—a claim Tertullian sharply rejected (*Against Marcion* 1.20.1). Against those who advocated continual seeking, Tertullian said that what may be an object of inquiry is only what does not impair the rule of faith (*Prescription Against Heretics* 12.5). The majority of believers affirm that "the rule of faith transfers [them] from a plurality of gods to the one and true God" (*Against Praxeas* 3.1). He concluded his summary of the rule of faith in *Prescription against Heretics* by saying that this rule was taught by Christ (13.1, 6). The apostles' teaching is equated with the rule of faith (*Prescription against Heretics* 26.9). Tertullian distinguished the rule of faith as preceding the rule of discipline, so the Adversary begins his work by adulterating the rule of faith and so adulterating the order of discipline (*On Monogamy* 2.3). The apostles, however, agreed on both the rules of faith and the rules of discipline (*On Modesty* 19.3).

The rule of faith had a definite form, was an object of faith, and constituted a law, as indicated by the statements that "its form exists in its proper order" and "faith has been deposited in the rule; it has a law (*lex*), and in its observance is salvation" (*Prescription against Heretics* 14). Indeed, Tertullian considered it comprehensive and complete: "to know nothing other than the rule is to know all things" (*Prescription against Heretics* 14). The rule covered conduct as well as doctrine: Some "depart from the rule of our discipline" (*Apology* 46.18).

Origen

The quotation in chapter 1 of Origen's account of essential Christian doctrines did not use the word "rule," but instead "apostolic teaching" and "church teaching." Origen had a rich variety of expressions for authoritative instruction. Such are "testimony of divine Scripture" (*On First Principles* 3.2.4), "ecclesiastical preaching" (*On First Principles* 3.1.1), "ecclesiastical discipline" (*Homilies on Joshua* 7.6), "ecclesiastical tradition" (*Commentary on Matthew* Series 46), "faith of the church" (*On First Principles* 1.6.1; 1.7.1), "ecclesiastical word" (*Commentary on Matthew* 11.17; 17.35), "ecclesiastical catechesis and teaching" (*Commentary on Matthew* 11.15; 15.7; cf. "ecclesiastical teaching of Jesus Christ" in *Commentary on Matthew* 10.14). In the *Homilies on Numbers*, Korah (Num 16) is a figure of those who revolt against the faith of the church and the teaching of the truth; heretics hold "ideas contrary to faith and the truth" (9.1). In the *Commentary on Romans,* Origen speaks of "ecclesiastical doctrine" (5.1.27), seems to take "measure of faith" (Rom 12:3) as equivalent to rule of faith (4.3.3), and in commenting on Romans 10:6 says that the church's rule establishes the necessity of baptism, according to John 3:5 (2.7.3). For Origen, the expressions apostolic, evangelical, and ecclesiastical appear to be interchangeable.[8]

Many of Origen's passages that do speak of the rule are in Latin translations for which the Greek does not survive. Such are "rule of truth" (*Homilies on Luke* 25.6), "apostolic rule of truth" (*Selections in the Psalms*, Hom. 4 on Ps 36:1), "the Christian rule" (*Commentary on Romans* 10.6). The "ecclesiastical discipline" is equated with "teaching of the church and the rule of the gospel" (*Homilies on Joshua* 7.6). "Rule of Scripture" and "rule of Christian truth" appear to be synonymous (*On First Principles* 3.3.4). "Rule of piety" is common in *On First Principles* (1.5.4; 3.1.7; 3.5.3; 4.3.14) and appears to have been a favorite of the translator Rufinus.

Where the Greek survives we have some significant statements employing the word "canon" (κανών). The word has the general sense of measure or norm.[9] Several of these passages associate it with the *church*, as in "canon of the majority in the church" (*Commentary on John* 13.16.98) and "canon of the heavenly church of Jesus Christ through the succession from the apostles" (*On First Principles* 4.2.2). One passage by way of allusion seems to equate the church's rule with the *Scriptures:* "according to the ecclesiastical canon, according to the purpose of the 'healthful teaching' [Titus 2:1 et al.]" (*Homilies on Jeremiah* 5.14.1). The same context provides some synonyms for canon: "words outside

8. Bardy, "La Règle de Foi d'Origéne," 193.

9. Van den Eynde, *Les Normes*, 304.

the word of truth, outside the word of the church." There is a similar combination in the *Commentary on Matthew*, where Scripture seems to be distinguished from the rule, although associated with it: "outside the faith and canon of the church and Scripture" (on Matt 22:34—27:63). Likewise in the *Dialogue with Heraclides*: "If there is lacking anything further concerning the canon [of faith], make mention of it; we shall speak yet more on the Scripture" (10).

A use of "canon" without further description occurs in the *Commentary on 1 Corinthians*, "When we transgress the canon by imagining to do something better, we depart from what is prescribed" (on 1 Corinthians 7:1–4). There were "precepts and canons delivered by the apostles" (*On Psalms* 64:5–6).

Canon is applied to a rule of conduct: Origen commented that Paul sent Tychicus to the church in Ephesus (Eph 6:21) to make known "the rule of his life and order of his deeds" (*Commentary on Ephesians* fragment 36).

The word *kanōn* (κανών) or "rule of faith" for Origen, as for Irenaeus and Tertullian, in general stood for the whole gospel or content of the Christian faith, the general belief of Christians. Origen's use of this word may be defined as "the belief generally held by the faithful in the church."[10]

Despite the deference shown in these passages to the rule adhered to by the church, Origen went against the general understanding of the resurrection of the flesh to argue for a spiritual body at the resurrection (e.g., *Against Celsus* 5.18–19; *Commentary on Matthew* 17.29).[11] However, he never consciously overruled Scripture.[12]

---

10. Hanson, *Origen's Doctrine of Tradition*, 91, 95.

11. Origen was often criticized for denying a resurrection of the flesh, but based on 1 Corinthians 15:44 he preferred to speak of a resurrection of a transformed, spiritual body.

12. Ibid., 107, 112.

In addition to the preface *On First Principles*, Origen has other summaries of essential Christian teaching, generally structured on the Trinity, as in 4.2.7. Thus in his *Commentary on John*, in explaining "all faith" (1 Cor 13:2), Origen says the following:

> First, it is necessary to believe in the only God who created all things and fashioned them and made them to exist out of what did not exist.
>
> Second, it is necessary also to believe that Jesus Christ is Lord and to believe everything relative to his divinity and humanity.
>
> Third, it is necessary to believe in the Holy Spirit, and in free will, that we are punished for our sins, and that we will be rewarded for doing well.
>
> Those who claim to believe in Jesus but do not believe that the God of the law and the gospel is one . . . and that the firmament is the work of his hands . . . omit a very important part of the faith.
>
> Or again, those who believe that he who was crucified under Pontius Pilate . . . was not born from the virgin Mary and the Holy Spirit but was born of Mary and Joseph lack things necessary to possessing all faith.
>
> And again, those who accept his divinity but take offense at his humanity . . . lack beliefs that are important for all faith.
>
> Or, on the contrary, those who accept the human things about him but reject his substantial existence as the Only-Begotten and First-born of all creation cannot say that they have all faith.
>
> (*Commentary on John* 32.187–93)

A briefer statement says, "If someone makes a pure and sincere declaration about the Father, the Only Begotten, and the Holy Spirit," and continues, "and likewise understands this about all rational creatures as made by God . . . but does not similarly affirm the resurrection of the flesh . . . [he has] polluted the holy flesh" (*Homilies on Leviticus* 5.10.3).

Against Celsus's charge that Christian dogma was a secret system, Origen affirms that the preaching of Christians (*kērugma Christianōn*/κήρυγμα Χριστιανῶν) was better known than the views of philosophers, and he summarizes Christian teaching: "The birth of Jesus from a virgin, his crucifixion, his resurrection in which many place their trust, and the judgment which is announced, bringing deserved punishment to sinners and a worthy reward to the righteous" (*Against Celsus* 1.7).

In the *Dialogue with Heraclides,* Origen began his inquiry by asking about the first two items of faith. He questioned Heraclides about whether he held the doctrine that "God is the Almighty, the uncreated, the supreme God who made all things." With Heraclides's affirmative answer, Origen proceeded, "Christ Jesus who was in the form of God, being other than the God in whose form he existed, was he God before he came in the body or not?"[13] With Heraclides's affirmation the discussion continued with further elements of Christology and the nature of the soul.

In a passage preserved in Latin, Origen refers to the "rule of Scriptures" as including:

> One God, who gave the Law and Gospel; also Christ Jesus firstborn of all creatures, who at the end of the ages according to the predictions of the prophets "came into the world" and received into himself the true nature of human flesh so that he submitted to birth from a virgin and

13. Translation by Henry Chadwick in Oulton and Chadwick, *Alexandrian Christianity*, 437–38.

received the death of the cross, and was raised
from the dead, and deified the human nature
that he had received; and also the Holy Spirit,
who was himself in the patriarchs and prophets,
who afterward was given in the apostles. And
they certainly believe in the resurrection of the
dead, even as the gospel teaches, and all things
whatever are related in the churches. . . . Christ,
who is Word and Truth, [warns against] being a
much worse judge, wandering away in doctrines
and not thinking according to the most accurate
rule of the Scriptures.

(*Commentary on Matthew* series 33 on Matt 24:4–5)[14]

Novatian

Novatian's preferred term, as in Irenaeus, was "rule of truth."
In addition to the passages quoted in chapter 1, note its oc-
currence in *On the Trinity* 11, 17, 21, and *On Jewish Foods*
7. The passages in *On the Trinity* have to do especially with
"the rule of truth concerning the person of Christ" (21), ar-
guing that as Son of God and Word of God he was fully God
and as Son of Man and Son of David he was fully human.

Augustine

Augustine represents the settled usage of "rule of faith" at
the end of Christian antiquity and established that terminology for Western Christianity in the succeeding centuries. He referred to "rule of faith" (*regula fidei*) or "rule of

---

14. A fragment from the *Commentary on Titus* is similar, only
stated negatively that the heretics hold other doctrines (*Patrologia
greaca*, edited by J.-P. Migne, 14.1303C–1306A).

truth" (*regula veritatis*) multiple times.[15] Following his conversion, Augustine affirmed, "I stood firm on that rule of faith" on which his mother had stood (*Confessions* 8.12.30).

Augustine's usage was greatly influenced by Tertullian,[16] but he took a step beyond Tertullian that was to be determinative for many later interpreters in explicitly equating the rule of faith with the baptismal confession of faith. He identified the rule of faith specifically with the baptismal creed (known as the "symbol") of the church at Milan, which he understood to be in general use in the churches.[17] Addressing those in his church at Hippo awaiting baptism a week later, he referred to the creed (the symbol or baptismal confession) that they had been taught, "which contains the brief and great rule of your faith, brief in words but great in content" (*Sermon* 59.1). Or again, "The symbol is a briefly summarized rule of faith" (*Sermon* 213.2).[18] In a sermon accompanying delivery of the creed that was to be memorized and later recited prior to baptism, Augustine said, "Receive, my sons, the rule of faith that is called the symbol," followed by the explanation that

15. Litfin, "The Rule of Faith in Augustine," 85, says about fifty times; Davidowski, "*Regula Fidei* in Augustine: Its Use and Function," 253, on the basis of a more nearly complete examination gives sixty-five times; by including related names, the number is given as around one hundred by Grech, "The *Regula Fidei* as a Hermeneutical Principle in Patristic Exegesis," 593, but the counting of Davidowski would make this cumulative figure too low.

16. Litfin, "The Rule of Faith in Augustine," 101.

17. At baptism a confession of faith was made either in a declaratory form, "I believe . . ." or in answer to questions, "Do you believe . . . ?" followed by an affirmation. This confession included Father, Son, Holy Spirit, and sometimes other items such as the church, the resurrection, and the life to come. It was often termed a "symbol," that is a "token," "badge," "marker of identification," or "pledge."

18. Edmund Hill reconstructs the creed from this sermon (Hill, *Sermons III/6 on the Liturgical Seasons*, 148).

these words are scattered through the divine Scriptures but are gathered and unified in the baptismal creed to aid the memory (*On the Symbol* [or *Creed*] 1.1). He further stated, "So this faith [the baptismal confession] is also a rule for salvation," followed by quotations of phrases in the symbol and Augustine's commentary on them (*Sermon* 215.2).

Augustine, as his predecessors, could use synonymous phrases for the rule of faith, some of which were common in earlier writers. In dealing with the question whether it was an angel or God that spoke to Moses in the burning bush, Augustine said that we should attempt to understand Scripture as a writer intended; however, "what we should never do is understand texts in a way that does not agree with the rule of faith, with the rule of truth, with the rule of piety" (*Sermon* 7.3). He urged his hearers, "Hold fast to the catholic church, and do not depart from the rule of truth" (*Exposition on the Psalms, Exposition 4 on Psalm 30*, 21.8).

In keeping with the extensive literary remains of Augustine he has an even more varied terminology than his predecessors. "Rule of truth" (*regula veritatis*) occurs about thirty times; truth for Augustine equals wisdom. "Rule of piety" (*regula pietatis*) (e.g., *On the Literal Interpretation of Genesis* 1) is the canon of the true philosophy, which is Christ. Other terms are "canonical rule" (*regula canonica*—only once, *The Trinity* 2.1.2), "apostolic rule" (*regula apostolica* (*On the One Baptism* 5.7), "catholic rule" (*regula catholica*—*Against Julian* 1.6), "rule of justice" *(regula iustitiae*—Augustine transformed the classical notion of justice to mean giving love to God and neighbor, as what was their due—*The Trinity* 8.6.9; *Explanation of the Psalms* 100.7), "sound doctrine" (*sana doctrina*—sixty-three times, used with *regula* in *Letter* 108.6 and *On Agreement among the Evangelists* 1.1.2, referring to the orthodox teaching of the catholic church, but a broader concept than rule of faith, including all that is involved in educating people in the knowledge of faith and love of God). All these terms are parallel to "rule of faith," but are not identical with it. Rule of faith is the only one of these terms used for the baptismal symbol.[19]

For Augustine, the rule of faith, the Scriptures, and the catholic church belonged together as a unified whole and were not to be set over against each other. He referred to "those who grow proud in evil opinions or some other cause of division and so depart from the rule of faith and from the communion of the catholic church and who refuse to accept the light of the holy Scriptures (which we call the New Testament) and the grace of the spiritual people of God" (*True Religion* 7.12).

Conclusion

There was not a fixed name in the second and third centuries for what is now called the rule of faith, nor was there a fixed wording for what it included. There was nonetheless a definite content, however varied the formulation of that content might be.

19. I take the information in this paragraph from Davidowski, "*Regula Fidei*," 260–95.

Table 1. Word Usage

	"Rule of faith"	"Rule of truth"	"Rule of piety"	"Ecclesiastical rule"
Dionysius of Corinth		X		
Polycrates	X			
Irenaeus	X	X		
Clement of Alexandria		X		X
Tertullian	X	X		
Hippolytus		X		
Origen	X	X	X	X
Novatian		X		
Victorius of Pettau	X			
Augustine	X	X	X	

Discussion Questions

1. What significance, if any, do you see in the fluidity of the terminology for the Rule of Faith? What significance, if any, do you see in the varied wordings of the Rule of Faith?

2. What distinction do you see between "Rule of Faith" and "canon of truth"?

3. Why did Clement of Alexandria have several equivalent expressions for Rule of Faith?

4. What terms did Origen use for authoritative statements of faith? What is the implication in each?

THREE

Interpretation of the Rule of Faith

The authors quoted before Augustine routinely describe the rule of faith as the preaching and teaching of the church, derived from Christ and handed down by the apostles to the church.[1] Apart from the Trinitarian structure, the accounts of the rule, especially in what is said about Christ, are quite similar to New Testament records of the apostolic preaching. C. H. Dodd outlined the apostle Paul's *kerygma*, as it can be recovered from his letters, as containing the following elements:

- The prophecies are fulfilled, and the new age is inaugurated by the coming of Christ.

- He was born of the seed of David.

- He died according to the Scriptures, to deliver us out of the present evil age.

- He was buried.

1. For passages connecting the rule of faith with the preaching and teaching of the church, see chapter 5.

- He rose on the third day, according to the Scriptures.
- He is exalted at the right hand of God, as Son of God and Lord of the living and the dead.
- He will come again as Judge and Savior of men.[2]

Dodd then proceeded to show these and related elements in the preaching recorded in Acts and their presence in the Gospels.

The heart of this apostolic preaching was the career of Jesus, particularly focused on his death, burial, and resurrection (1 Cor 15:3–5). The rule of faith was the continuation of these summaries of main elements in the gospel, set in the larger context of faith in God and the church's experience of the Holy Spirit.

Acts of Justin

Justin's brief statement of his faith to the magistrate in Rome expresses the twin pillars of early Christian doctrine: (a) the one God, Creator of all that is, and (b) his Son, the Lord Jesus Christ predicted by the prophets of the Old Testament.

Irenaeus

The centerpiece of Irenaeus's thought is the passage in *Against Heresies* 1.10 quoted in chapter 1. Its position shows it to be the standard by which he judged the "Gnosis Falsely So-Called" against which he was writing.[3] The centrality of

2. Dodd, *The Apostolic Preaching and its Developments*, 17.

3. Thomas C. K. Ferguson finds that Irenaeus's exposition and critique of two Gnostic systems run inseparably parallel in 1.1–8 and 1.11–21, with the rule of truth in 1.10 as the centerpiece of his confutation (T. C. K.Fergusson, "The Rule of Truth and Irenaean Rhetoric in Book 1 of *Against Heresies*," 356, 358).

the rule of truth/faith for Irenaeus is shown in the *Demonstration of the Apostolic Preaching*, which indeed may be seen as an exposition of the rule of faith.[4]

Irenaeus set the apostolic preaching in a trinitarian framework. His statement in *Against Heresies* 1.10 sets forth three elements of the theology central to the refutation of Gnosticism: (a) the one God who is Creator, (b) the salvation of the flesh through the incarnation of Christ, and (c) the revealing of this plan through the life of Christ as put forth in Scripture.[5]

Irenaeus has other three-fold summaries of the Christian faith besides *Against Heresies* 1.10 and *Demonstration* 6.

> [The spiritual disciple] has complete faith in one God Almighty, from whom are all things; and a strong conviction in the Son of God, Jesus Christ our Lord, through whom are all things, and in his dispensations by which the Son of God became a human being; and in the Spirit of God, who presents a knowledge of the truth, who sets forth the dispensations of the Father and the Son to dwell among human beings in each generation even as the Father wills.
>
> (*Against Heresies* 4.33.7)

> Having the firm tradition from the apostles, giving us to see that the faith of all is one and the same, since all receive one and the same God, and believe in the same dispensation of the incarnation of the Son of God, and know the same gift of the Spirit, and are devoted to the same

4. Blowers, "The *Regula Fidei* and the Narrative Character of Early Christian Faith," 212.

5. T. C. K. Ferguson, "The Rule of Truth and Irenaean Rhetoric in Book 1 of *Against Heresies*," 374.

> commandments, and observe the same form in
> the arrangements with regard to the church, and
> expect the same advent of the Lord, and main-
> tain the same salvation of the whole person, that
> is of soul and body.
>
> (*Against Heresies* 5.20.1)

One may compare the interpretation of Psalm 45:7–8 as
speaking of the Son, being God, receiving from the Father
God the oil of anointing, which is the Spirit (*Demonstration*
47).

Even more frequent are binary summaries of the faith,
mentioning only the Father and the Son. False teachers
"take captive from the truth those who do not maintain a
firm faith in the one God the Father Almighty and in the
one Lord Jesus Christ the Son of God" (*Against Heresies*
1.3.6). The apostles "all delivered to us that there is one
God, Maker of heaven and earth, announced by the law and
the prophets, and one Christ Son of God" (*Against Heresies*
3.1.2). The passage from 3.4.2 quoted in chapter 1 is typical
in giving greater elaboration to the career of Christ than to
the work of the Father. More attention is given to God in
another passage, but including the following words:

> John, the disciple of the Lord, preaches this faith
> . . . to persuade them that there is one God who
> made all things by his Word . . . . By the Word
> by whom God made the creation he also offered
> salvation to human beings who are in the cre-
> ation. . . . According to the opinion of no one of
> the heretics was the Word of God made flesh.
>
> (*Against Heresies* 3.11.1, 3)[6]

"We have shown that there is one God the Father and one
Christ Jesus our Lord, who came by a universal dispensation

---

6. See another statement from this passage quoted in chapter 2.

and recapitulated all things in himself [Eph 1:10]" (*Against Heresies* 3.16.6). "Therefore, the Father revealed himself to all, by making his Word visible to all; and, in turn, the Word revealed the Father and the Son, since he was seen by all," and the passage continues by saying, "By the creation itself the Word reveals God the Creator" (*Against Heresies* 4.6.5).

Irenaeus consistently identifies God the Father as the Creator. This was traditional, but the emphasis was dictated by the distinction that Marcion made between the Creator God of the Old Testament and the Father of Jesus Christ and by the Gnostics's demotion of the Creator (the Demiurge) to a lesser being than the supreme God. The Holy Spirit is presented as the one who prophesied the coming of Christ through the prophets, produced a recognition of the truth, led human beings in the path of justice, and in the new age was poured out in a new manner to renew humanity to God.

Otherwise, Irenaeus's accounts of the preaching of the church give fuller development to the career of Christ. He includes the following items:

- the Word as the one through whom God created all things,

- his becoming incarnate through the virgin birth in order to restore humanity to communion with God,

- his suffering under Pontius Pilate,

- his resurrection,

- his bodily ascension,

- and his coming again for a general resurrection and judgment, bringing eternal punishment to the ungodly and eternal life to the faithful.

In Irenaeus and others, the consistently fuller statements about Christ—structured according to his career from

pre-existence through his earthly ministry, death and resurrection, to his coming again for judgment—have suggested that these statements of the rule of truth/faith resulted
from a conflation of the *kerygma* (the proclamation about
Christ) with a trinitarian formula (likely derived from baptism—Matt 28:19).

From the statements in Irenaeus, several points relative to the rule of faith may be determined.[7] (1) The affirmation of its apostolic origin and its association with baptism
(*Against Heresies* 1.9.4—1.10.1; *Demonstration* 6–7). The
trinitarian structure likely derives from the baptismal formula (Matt 28:19) and the preceding confession of faith.
(2) Although the wording reflects emerging creeds, the
expanded article of Christ reflects the early *kerygma*.[8] (3)
The one God and one Lord pattern is early (1 Cor 8:6; cf.
1 Clement 46.6 with the addition of "one Spirit"). (4) The
wording was flexible but followed a distinct outline. (5) The
rule was often associated with Scripture and the apostolic
tradition transmitted through Scripture. The rule was an
epitome, the essential content, of the Scriptural tradition,
an abstract of the biblical plan of salvation.[9] (6) The formulation could focus on the two articles of the Father and
the Son or on three articles with the inclusion of the Holy
Spirit. The structure and traditional elements of the rule in
Irenaeus indicate its contents preceded his polemical use of
it (chapter 5).

7. I follow here Bokedal, "The Rule of Faith: Tracing Its Origins,"
but with modifications.

8. Before the third and fourth centuries, what are sometimes
called creeds were confessions of faith without a fixed wording or
official sanction and employed in various contexts.

9. On this point, Blowers, "The *Regula Fidei*," 207, 209.

Tertullian

Tertullian—similarly to Irenaeus, but less decidedly so—set the rule of faith in a trinitarian framework, yet with primary attention to the Father and the Son. His wording of the contents, again like Irenaeus, varied in his different presentations, but followed a broadly similar outline. And, again like Irenaeus, he maintained a unity of Scripture, tradition, and the catholic church; but, in his later writings, Scripture and the new revelations from the Paraclete (Spirit) took precedence. He used "rule of faith" in a broad sense for the whole content of the Christian faith, but in three passages he gave a specific summary of the faith.[10] In *Prescription of Heretics* 13 and *Veiling of Virgins* 1 there is a two-part structure with an emphasis on the history of Christ, which particularly in the former determines the order of presentation, not the Trinity; there is a more tripartite structure in *Against Praxeas* 2.

The sequence of the rule—moving from creation to the prophets, to the gospel, to the giving of the Spirit, to the church, and finally to the eschaton—is the framework of Tertullian's *Against Marcion*. The biblical narrative was an overarching story centered on Christ that provided the touchstone of Tertullian's faith and his understanding of Scripture.[11]

Tertullian begins each of his three accounts of the rule with the one God, who is Creator of the universe out of nothing. In each case he moves quickly to the Son of God, and in two of the three accounts identifies the Word (an indication, I take it, of prior Greek sources) as the means of creation and in one account explains that by the Word God

10. Countryman, "Tertullian and the *Regula Fidei*," 208–210.

11. Litfin, "Tertullian's Use of the *Regula Fidei* as an Interpretive Device in *Adversus Marcionem*," 408–9.

brought the universe into being out of nothing. All three accounts mention Christ's birth from a virgin, his suffering or crucifixion, his resurrection, and his coming again as judge. The fuller account in *Prescription of Heretics* 13 includes his appearances to the patriarchs, his speaking through the prophets, his miracles during his personal ministry, and his burial. That account and *Against Praxeas* 2 add that Christ sent the Holy Spirit as a guide and sanctifier of believers.

The rule of faith was a norm for believing, but in the phrase "rule of faith," faith was not an objective genitive. The faith, the contents of the rule, constituted the rule. The confession made at baptism (the symbol or creed) was made according to the rule of faith. "We enter the water and profess the Christian faith in the words of its rule" (*On Shows* 4). We should not, however, *equate* the rule of faith with the creed, for Tertullian's statements of the rule (as is true for other statements) contain points not found in any known creed.[12] There is an overlap in contents, but the functions were different (more on this in chapter 5).

Origen

It is notable that in *On First Principles* and elsewhere, Origen used summaries of the faith as starting points for his own speculations. The basic facts of the Christian faith are everywhere taken as a given. He moved from faith to philosophy, not in the opposite direction.[13]

Origen included in his list of necessary doctrines topics not found in other accounts of the rule of faith. His listing was dictated by his distinction between doctrines clearly taught and those subject to theological speculation.

---

12. Van den Eynde, *Les Normes*, 297.
13. Outler, "Origen and the *Regulae Fidei*," 220–21.

Some doctrines were necessary for all Christians to believe, and some were for the wise and learned to explore.[14] This distinction corresponds to the distinction Origen made between the simple believers, to whom belong the elementary dogmas, and the perfect, to whom belong allegorical explanations.[15] The first criterion of orthodoxy was acceptance of the elementary doctrines.

Origen's account of fundamental doctrines included the nature of the soul, existence of demons and angels, free will, the creation of the world in time, and the inspired Scriptures requiring allegorical interpretation—items not in other accounts of the rule of faith. On the other hand, it omitted terminology sometimes present in other accounts and used by Origen in other contexts: Almighty for the Father, Pontius Pilate as the one under whom Christ suffered, Christ seated at the right hand of the Father. On those points mentioned by Origen he gives a rather elaborate description. Indeed this statement was too long and too complex to think that Origen was reporting some liturgical, catechetical, or baptismal formula. It was *his own* formulation of the teachings handed down by the church.[16] The same is true of the formulations by the other authors we have quoted. Pamphilius's *Apology* notably entitles the passage "Catalogue of the Ecclesiastical Preaching," recognizing that it was a statement of the church's preaching and not a confessional or creedal statement.[17] Although some passages in

14. Bardy, "La Règle de Foi d'Origéne," 183–89.

15. Ibid., 196.

16. Bardy's statement (ibid., 189) that the passage is not properly speaking a rule of faith, since it had no official value and represents only the personal thought of Origen, is gratuitous, for neither were other statements of the rule.

17. Ibid., 189.

Origen look like a creed or to be based on a creed, Origen did not identify the rule of faith with a creed.[18]

Origen's full account of the apostolic preaching in *On First Principles* elaborates on the work of God. He not only created the universe out of nothing but also set it in order. He was God of the patriarchs and righteous persons of the Old Testament. Then, in accordance with prophecy, he sent the Lord Jesus Christ for the calling of Jews and Gentiles. As a further thrust against Marcion and the Gnostics this creator God is affirmed to be both good and just, the Father of the Lord Jesus Christ, the giver of the Law, the Prophets, and the Gospels, and the God of the apostles and of the Old and New Testaments.

The expanded description of the Lord Jesus Christ affirms that he ministered to the Father in the creation. Then in the last days he was made flesh, taking a body like other human beings, being born of the virgin and the Holy Spirit, and so becoming man as well as God. His sufferings were real and not feigned, for he died a common death. After his resurrection he associated with his disciples before being taken up to heaven.

The Holy Spirit is united with the Father and the Son. The same Spirit inspired the prophets and the apostles.

The items Origen included in his account of essential doctrines in addition to Father, Son, and Holy Spirit include some of his special concerns, such as the nature of the soul (having a substance of its own, rational, and at the resurrection of the dead receiving either blessedness or fire according to its deeds), free will (so human beings are not controlled by fate but choose either a wise and righteous life or one of sin and evil),[19] demons (who are real beings

18. R. P. C. Hanson discusses the relation of the rule of faith to the creed in Origen (*Origen's Doctrine*, 114–21).

19. Jackson, "Sources of Origen's Doctrine of Freedom."

in service of the devil and war against the soul in order to weigh it down with sins),[20] and the belief that the Scriptures were composed under the inspiration of God's Spirit and contain in addition to their obvious meaning hidden mysteries.

Unfortunately this important passage survives only in Latin translation and some of its wording is suspect as coming from the translator rather than from Origen himself. The substance of the teaching, nonetheless, is supported by other statements in Origen's voluminous writings.

The rule of faith represented the church's public teaching and so was not distinguished from the *kerygma*. It was distinct from Scripture but closely related to it, for it represented the church's interpretation of Scripture, but was not a separate source of doctrine from Scripture. Origen never professes to derive even his advanced doctrine from anywhere but the Bible.[21] At the heart of his summaries of the faith of the church are the facts of the life of Jesus, and, however much Origen moved beyond them, they emphasize the historical roots of the Christian faith.

Other Writings

The treatise *Against Noetus* attributed to Hippolytus refutes the teaching of Noetus concerning the relation of God and Christ. In defending a strict monotheism but believing in the divinity of Christ, Noetus taught a form of Modalism, namely that God the Father and God the Son were different modes of manifestation of the One God. The result was that the one born of the virgin and who died on the cross was one and the same person with the one God who was

---

20. Everett Feguson, "Origen's Demonology."

21. Hanson, *Origen's Doctrine*, 91–92, 95, 101, 112.

Creator. Hence, the concern of this treatise was to mark the *distinction* of the two persons, but the Holy Spirit is included as well in the exposition: "The Father indeed is one, but there are two Persons, because there is also the Son; and then there is the third, the Holy Spirit" (*Against Noetus* 14). Otherwise, the facts asserted by the presbyters at Smyrna and Hippolytus follow the same outline usual in statements identified as the rule of faith. There is one God, but most is said about Christ his Son. The Father has a Word through whom he made all things and who was preached in the Law and Prophets. This divine Word came down from heaven and took flesh from the virgin Mary, becoming all that belongs to the human condition (except for sin) in order to bring salvation to all. Being formed from the virgin and the Holy Spirit, he was God in a body, a perfect human being in reality and not in mere appearance. After his suffering and resurrection, he appeared to the disciples, breathed on them the Holy Spirit, was seen taken up in a cloud to heaven where he sits at the right hand of the Father. He is coming again as judge of all the living and the dead. Hippolytus closes his treatise with a doxology to Christ, the Father, and the Holy Spirit, with the added note that this glory is given in the holy church.

The *Didascalia Apostolorum* is included primarily to show that the same faith exhibited in Latin and Greek sources was held in early Syriac-speaking Christianity. The passage quoted from the conclusion identifies Christ as the Nazarene, crucified under Pontius Pilate. It has the added feature of including the dead Christ's sojourn in Hades, where he declares the gospel to the righteous dead of Old Testament times. Christ's resurrection is a guarantee of the resurrection of others. The ascension was by the power and Spirit of God. He is coming again to judge the living and the dead. This work too closes with a doxology, but it mentions only the Father and the Son.

Novatian's discussion is explicitly trinitarian and represents an advance and systematization of what is found in Irenaeus and Tertullian before him. His descriptions of God the Father and Jesus Christ the Son were already traditional by his time in the mid-third century. God the Father is the all-powerful Creator of all things. As was characteristic, the longest treatment is given to Jesus Christ. The distinctive feature of Novatian's account (but again with ample precedent in other contexts in earlier writers, notably Justin Martyr's *Dialogue with Trypho* and Irenaeus's *Demonstration of the Apostolic Preaching*) is the accumulation of prophecies in regard to each of the main features of what is said about Christ. Novatian represents an advance in the fuller treatment he gives to the work of the Holy Spirit, not only inspiring Scripture, but also giving spiritual gifts to the church, giving rebirth in baptism, effecting holiness in believers, and through apostles, martyrs, virgins, and others giving testimony to Christ and rebuking heretics and the wicked.

Despite its later date than the other quoted sources, Victorinus of Pettau's *Commentary on the Apocalypse* 11.1 reflects an early binitarian exposition, mentioning the Holy Spirit only as the gift of the risen Christ. Victorinus takes the "reed" of the Revelation 11:1 used to measure the temple of God as the measure of faith. He anticipates Augustine in identifying the statement of the faith with what was confessed rather than what was preached. Like Hippolytus, Victorinus emphasizes that the Son of God in becoming incarnate had a real human soul and body. In this later statement we encounter the perspective that "we confess" this faith rather than this was the faith preached and delivered to us.

Discussion Questions

1. What early Christian author's treatment of the Rule of Faith is most appealing to you? Why?

2. Distinguish Rule of Faith from a creed, Scripture, and tradition.

3. Compare the Rule of Faith with accounts of apostolic preaching in the New Testament.

4. Why does the career of Christ occupy greater space in the Rule of Faith than statements of the Father and of the Holy Spirit?

5. Do Christians in general think of the events of the end time as essential to their faith? If so, or not, Why?

FOUR

Studies of the Rule of Faith

Early in the twentieth century W. P. Patterson sketched three classic theories of the rule of faith: (1) the Roman Catholic/Eastern Orthodox view of revelation through Scripture and tradition with an ecclesiastical organ for binding authority (the papacy for Roman Catholics and the ecumenical councils and patriarchs for the Orthodox),[1] (2) the old Protestant view of "Scripture alone" interpreted by theological systems, and (3) the rationalistic approach that set reason as the authority. Patterson further points out that liberal Protestantism has been shaped by Friedrich Schleirmacher, who taught the priority of religious feeling, and Albrecht Ritschl, who combined reason with personal faith in the gospel that gives the experience of salvation.[2]

1. Coan, *The Rule of Faith in the Ecclesiastical Writings of the First Two Centuries* (1924) represents the pre-Vatican II Roman Catholic view. He uses "rule of faith" for source of authority, and he holds a tendentious view of the Protestant position as private interpretation, which he equates with heresy.

2. Patterson, *The Rule of Faith* (1912), 9–22.

Our concern in this chapter will be historical rather than theological, as we survey scholarly studies aimed at determining the rule of faith according to early Christian literature.

C. P. Caspari laid the foundation of modern studies of the rule of faith with an extensive collection of the sources for it.[3] He concluded that the church at Rome had a fixed confession of faith used at baptism by the middle of the second century, a conclusion accepted by Harnack (below), but he did not connect it with the rule of faith. August Hahn's much used compilation[4] is based on Caspari.

Apart from these collections, a survey of modern studies of the rule of faith may appropriately begin with the influential work of Theodor Zahn and Adolf von Harnack in the late nineteenth and early twentieth centuries. Zahn began where Augustine left off in identifying the rule of faith with the baptismal confession of faith.[5] The varied wordings of the rule of faith and variety of titles in different authors were due to their freely alluding to the confession of faith with the confidence that baptized believers would recognize its origin and its basic importance. He plainly stated his position, "The rule of faith is identical with the baptismal confession."[6]

---

3. Caspari, *Ungedruckte, unbeachtete und wenig beachtete Quellen zur Geschichte des Taufsymbols und der Glaubensregel* (3 vols. 1866–75) and *Alte und neue Quellen zur Geschichte des Taufsymbols und der Glaubensregel* (1879).

4. Hahn, *Bibliothek der Symbole und Glaubensregeln der alten Kirche* (1897).

5. For Zahn and the other early students of this period see Armstrong, "From the κανὼν τῆς ἀληθείας to the κανὼν τῶν γραφῶν" (2010), 32–43.

6. Zahn, "Glaubensregel und Taufbekenntnis in der alten Kirche" (1881).

Whereas for Zahn the rule of faith was regarded as the liturgical profession of faith (the symbol), for Harnack and Kattenbusch it was the confession of faith interpreted in an anti-heretical sense. Harnack, although acknowledging that "Zahn was virtually right when he says . . . that the rule of faith is the baptismal confession," modified his theory. The "rule of truth" for Irenaeus was the "old baptismal confession well known to the communities" for which he wrote. Harnack went further in trying to situate the rule of faith in a historical context. In a broader sense the apostolic tradition, consisting of everything traced back to Christ through the medium of the apostles, but especially the history and words of Jesus, formed the content of the faith, the "canon of faith" or "canon of truth." Hence, the early statements of the preaching of the apostles combined with the trinitarian baptismal confession of faith were formulated as anti-heretical rules of faith by Irenaeus and Tertullian. The Roman church had taken the lead in codifying a precisely formulated baptismal confession.[7]

Ferdinand Kattenbusch's analysis of previous studies solidified acceptance of Zahn's position. In contrast to Harnack, he saw a distinction between Irenaeus and Tertullian on the relation of the rule of faith to the baptismal symbol. Irenaeus did not clearly distinguish between the rule of truth and the confession recited by the candidate at baptism, but Tertullian does recognize a difference. Nonetheless, he adopted the view that the rule of faith should be identified with the confession of faith made at baptism.[8]

Johannes Kunze accepted the association of the rule of faith with the baptismal confession but challenged their identity. Zahn did not adequately recognize that the early

7. Harnack, *History of Dogma* (1900), 1.157–58; 2.20–32, 151.

8. Kattenbusch, *Das Apostolische Symbol* (2 vols. 1894, 1900), 1.20–21; 2.83.

catholic fathers needed an authoritatively interpreted baptismal confession and a definitively formulated statement of the apostolic teaching in order to exclude Gnostic views. Harnack failed to recognize the relationship of the rule of faith and the canon of the Scriptures. Kunze concluded that eventually the rule of faith became the canon of the Scriptures. From the late second century to the early fourth, the baptismal confession was not uniform in the churches. Although the *regula* and the symbol are very near to each other, the latter was formulated for the church and the rule of faith was an anti-heretical instrument. They are not identical, for each specimen of the rule of faith contains elements not included in any baptismal formula. The rule of faith was not another name for the baptismal confession. Rather, "The symbol is the rule of faith in summary form."[9]

Valdemar Ammundsen, a Danish scholar, gave to the English-speaking world a different perspective. He showed that "rule of truth" in Irenaeus means *truth itself* is the canon and refers to the main, unambiguous content of Scripture. Whereas book 3 of *Against Heresies* is often taken to mean that Irenaeus takes his stand on tradition or the baptismal creed, the passages rightly understood say the opposite. A true tradition transmitted by the living voice is an assertion of the Gnostics. Irenaeus follows the Gnostics to the battleground they prefer, tradition outside Scripture, and refutes them on their own ground. The foundation of faith is the gospel in Scripture. His examination of all the passages using "rule of truth" produced the following results: (1) The rule of truth is not an institution, formula, or book, but genuine apostolic Christianity. (2) It was not a formal rule, but a body of doctrine. (3) The rule is truth itself. (4) Truth has a central place in the theology of Irenaeus—truth

9. Kunze, *Glaubensregel, Heilige Schrift und Taufbekenntnis* (1899), 2–3, 23, 72, 75, 79–80.

leads to salvation. The rule was not formed against heretics, but excludes heresy as truth excludes error. (5) Truth is first found in Scripture. (6) The same truth may be found outside Scripture in the tradition of the church, but Irenaeus never calls tradition the rule of truth. (7) It is quite doubtful that there is a formulated creed in Irenaeus.[10]

Gustav Bardy's study of Origen's terminology went further than Ammundsen and determined that "canon" in Origen referred to *the biblical canon*. In Origen's varied terminology "it is solely a question of the books of the Old and New Testament." "The Scriptures themselves constitute the inviolable rule that directs the believer." The rule of faith is found in the Scriptures; outside of Scripture there is no question of knowing the rule of faith. Origen did not use *kanōn* to designate a rule of faith or symbol imposed on the faithful in the name of the church, but he "habitually understood by this term the canon of the inspired Scriptures."[11] Dogmas that are at the base of the teaching of the church Origen names "the ecclesiastical preaching." Bardy notes that where the Greek exists it is not favorable to Origen's Latin translator. He grants that in the *Commentary on Romans* there appears to be a baptismal symbol, but suggests that we may see here a formula of Rufinus. Moreover, the content of tradition is nothing other than what is found in the canon of the Scriptures and refers to the teaching of the apostles transmitted by the church.[12]

Damien Van den Eynde understood the rule of truth in the early Fathers as the whole of doctrine, considered

10. Ammundsen, "The Rule of Truth in Irenaeus" (1912).

11. Bardy, "La Règle de Foi d'Origéne" (1919), 162–96. The Alexandrians' emphasis on Scripture continued later: Isidore of Pelusium declared, although not exclusively, "The rule of truth, I mean the divine Scriptures" (*Epistles* 4.114).

12. Bardy, "La Règle," 194, 195.

immutable, that distinguished the churches from heresies. It was not the symbol, as Zahn, Harnack, and others thought, nor was it to be identified with apostolic tradition or Scripture as Kunze and R. Seeberg wanted it to be. It was the content of revelation, the principal and invariable part of the deposit of doctrine in the written word and tradition. Around the center that constitutes the rule of faith are (1) doctrines of lesser importance, (2) the rule of discipline, and (3) secret doctrines in Clement of Alexandria and others. He affirms the catholic view that Scripture is subordinate to the living tradition.[13]

Albert C. Outler approached the usage of Origen by noting the distinction between the baptismal confession and the rules of faith. The baptismal symbol was a liturgical formula of initiation and relatively rigid in form; *regulae* were minimum statements of the common faith. These all repeat the facts of the life of Jesus and emphasize the historical rootage of the Christian faith. Distinguishing places where the tradition was clear from places where legitimate speculation was possible, Origen turned these summaries of the common faith into starting points for his own theologizings.[14]

Bengt Hägglund, after a thorough examination of Irenaeus, Tertullian, and Clement of Alexandria, emphasized that the *regula* was not identical with the symbol nor with a definite interpretation of the symbol.[15] The concept refers to the whole teaching of the church, the teaching proclaimed by apostles and prophets and formulated in Scripture. The baptismal confession (as a short summary of the contents

13. Van den Eynde, *Les Normes de l'Enseignement Chrétien* (1933), 281–22.

14. Outler, "Origen and the *Regulae Fidei*" (1939), 212–221.

15. Hägglund, "Die Bedeutung der *'regula fidei'* als Grundlage theologischer Aussagen" (1958), 3–4, 34–40.

of revelation), Holy Scripture, and apostolic tradition were *all* included in the rule of faith/truth, but it was not identical with any of them. He draws the following conclusions concerning the rule of faith as the foundation of theological declarations: (1) The *regula* presupposes that the content of Christian faith from the beginning formed a unity and involved a harmony of the Old and New Testaments. (2) It presupposes that this content is definite and always remains the same; doctrine may develop only insofar as the basic content is unchanged. (3) Truth means reality in opposition to appearance or human discovery or ideas, but especially true knowledge of God and salvation. (4) The truth of saving history is the beginning point of the church's tradition and the plumb line for judging true or false doctrine. (5) The task of the church's dogma is to transmit the tradition one time given by revelation.

Pieter Smulders confirmed the distinction between rules of faith and creedal confessions of faith. He presented in chart form a comprehensive comparison of statements of the rule of faith, including passages not expressly designated by the names usually employed, but containing similar content. Although not finding direct antecedents of the rule of faith in the New Testament, he characterized the basic pattern of the rules as "a highly archaic scheme of kerygmatic preaching."[16]

Dieter Lührmann considered the relation of the rule of faith to the canon of Scripture. The criteria for canonicity were apostolicity and agreement with the *regula fidei*, and these two belong together. The rule was a summary of the original doctrine of the apostles, which is presented in

16. Smulders, "Some Riddles in the Apostles` Creed, II. Creeds and Rules of Faith" (1971), 366.

Scripture. What is apostolic can only be what corresponds to the *regula fidei*. It formed the "canon of the canon."[17]

L. William Countryman advanced an oral-social theory of the origin of the *regula fidei*. He promoted the thesis that the *regula* was used in catechesis. It provided a course outline to be expanded in communicating basic Christian doctrine. The bishop provided the model of instruction for his catechists. Tertullian could then use it for an anti-heretical purpose. Tertullian held to a unity of Scripture, tradition, and the catholic church.[18]

William R. Farmer found the terminology of Galatians 2:14 and 6:16 as the exegetical basis for the formulation of a "canon (*regula*) of faith," and Marcion alone as the one who had a strong reason to bring these texts into the exegetical tradition. It is plausible that Marcion's use of Galatians and the church's response played an important role in the second-century development of the *regula fidei*.[19] I note that this study has to do with the usage of the terminology, not necessarily with an anti-heretical purpose of the rule.

Eric Osborn emphasized the place of reason in the rule of faith. The philosophical background was more important than the legal for understanding the *regula*. Osborn showed how Irenaeus, Clement of Alexandria, and Tertullian each in his own way argued *for* the rule of faith, argued *by* the rule of faith, and argued *from* the rule of faith. Having established the link between the rule and the arguments of these early writers, Osborn concludes that the rule did not limit reason to make room for faith but used faith to make

17. Dieter Lührmann, "Gal 2:9 und die katholischen Briefe: Bemerkungen zum Kanon und zur regula fidei," *Zeitschrift für die neuentestamentliche Wissenschaft* 73 (1981):65–87.

18. Countryman, "Tertullian and the *Regula Fidei*" (1982).

19. Farmer, "Galatians and the Second-Century Development of the *Regula Fidei*" (1984), 153, 179.

room for reason. Without a credible first principle, reason was lost in an infinite regress. The success of the second century was the affirmation that there was a true gospel, and this was more important than any particular account of that gospel.[20]

Whereas Harnack and others had seen the baptismal creed as coming first and the rule of faith as commentary on it, more recent studies that correlate the rule of faith with a creed reverse the order and see the creed as condensing and codifying the contents of the rule.[21]

Paul Blowers used the statements of the *regula* to emphasize the narrative character of early Christian faith. His survey of earlier scholarship showed the formation of the rule occurred in the context of a basic struggle for Christian identity with a focus on its narrative and dramatic dimension. The Christian narrative was both immutable and subject to varied presentations. No rendition of the rule could alter the apostolic faith, but its exposition was naturally varied. Irenaeus's use of *hypothesis* (ὑπόθεσις—*Against Heresies* 1.9.4) is best understood as "storyline" or "plot." The rule was not an "epic" but was an epitome of the scriptural tradition. This narrative structure of the rule carried over into the creeds; although the latter collapsed the history, confessing the creed brought one into its story. This narrative structure of Christian faith shaped Christian identity. The struggle with Gnosticism was a contest of "our story versus theirs." The *regula* was authoritative for early

20. Osborn, "Reason and the Rule of Faith in the Second Century AD" (1989).

21. For example, Frances Young, *The Making of the Creeds* (1991), 9, that the rule of faith at the end of the second century was a summary of the faith—not fixed, but adaptable to various situations—and a precursor of creeds.

Christians because it preserved a particular *story* as the canon of faith.[22]

The use of the rule of faith in interpretation of Scripture has been an important theme of recent study. Prosper S. Grech dealt with the *regula fidei* as a hermeneutical principle in patristic exegesis. He raised the questions, Is pre-comprehension a preunderstanding or a prejudice? Does a hermeneutical principle render Scripture more comprehensible or is it superimposed on the Bible? Against the Gnostics, Irenaeus gave some rules of interpretation: a text must not be taken from its literary context; the broader context of the Old and New Testament must be taken into account; ambiguous texts are to be interpreted by clear texts; the meaning must conform to the rule of faith, which synthesizes the public tradition received through the succession of bishops [presbyters]. The rule of faith is a genuine preunderstanding of the biblical texts because it stems from the same source. The real ground of belief is Scripture; tradition contributes to its right understanding. Clement of Alexandria added to Irenaeus's concept of context "symbolic reason." Origen distinguished doctrines accepted as certain from others still open to research and dispute. He is a witness to the rule as a criterion for the interpretation of the Bible. Tertullian did not belittle Scripture in favor of the rule, but Scripture should be read in the context of the rule. Ancient practices of a liturgical nature not contradicted by Scripture can also be considered apostolic because of their antiquity. Tertullian extended tradition to include ritual, but this is subject to change. Grech continued his survey into the fourth and fifth centuries. For Basil of Caesarea liturgical practices may derive from the oral, private teaching of the apostles inherited by tradition (*On*

22. Blowers, "The *Regula Fidei* and the Narrative Character of Early Christian Faith" (1997).

the Holy Spirit 27). The Gnostic crisis was over; otherwise this argument would have been a two-edged sword cutting against the church. By the time of Augustine the contents of the rule had been broadened. The rule of faith received at baptism was the creed. Even creeds could be misinterpreted and did not address recent controversies. Hence, Augustine appealed to liturgical practices, such as infant baptism as a witness to the inheritance of Adam's sin; he also appealed to the testimony of older fathers and the authority of plenary councils. He had respect for the *sensus fidelium* (mind of the faithful). Among Augustine's rules of interpretation was the principle, than an interpretation contrary to the rule is to be rejected, but any interpretation the rule does not contradict is allowable. Vincent of Lérins summarized the situation in the fifth century. In sum, Grech says that the rule was to safeguard Scripture, not replace it.[23]

Some recent studies still maintain an association of the rule of faith with the confession of faith. Catherine González recognized that for Irenaeus and Tertullian the rule of faith was the sum of the gospel message and that elaboration was possible at almost every point when the situation demanded it. The rule had a variety of functions: baptismal confession, catechetical instruction, approval of those to be ordained as clergy. It gave identity in the face of heresies and unity in spite of diverse theologies. Much of her treatment is a historical survey through the twentieth century, when creedal forms tended to become personal, individual statements of faith, rather than statements of the church's faith. Failing to observe the distinction between the early rule of faith and creeds, perhaps still under the influence of earlier studies that identified the rule with the baptismal confession, she blends the idea of a rule of faith

23. Grech, "The *Regula Fidei* as a Hermeneutical Principle in Patristic Exegesis" (1998).

with creeds, as in the statement that for the Western church the most familiar form of the rule of faith is the Apostles Creed.[24]

Ephraim Radner and George Sumner's edited work on *The Rule of Faith: Scripture, Canon, and Creed in a Critical Age* is mostly concerned with the modern theological relevance of the articles of the Apostles' Creed.[25] Their introduction affirms that the canon of Scripture and the creed are the "rule of faith." Canon and creed are inseparable.

L. H. Westra brought the apocryphal *Acts of Peter* into the discussion of the rule of faith. He cites several passages that refer to topics in the Old Roman Creed, but in a somewhat or even quite different formulation, so there is no quotation or borrowing from that creed. Rather these passages may be connected with the *regula fidei*, the characteristics of which are a short summary of the faith, worded freely, and stated in a polemical context. The *Acts of Peter* witness to a *regula fidei* of markedly conservative character. Certain features seem to point to North Africa as their home.[26] In spite of the title of the article, most of the cited passages are in a kerygmatic context, and none is in a confessional setting.

David Henderson's brief treatment does not have a new contribution to make. He rightly notes that the rule of faith for Irenaeus was nothing other than the truth the apostles had deposited in the church to be handed down by the succession of pastors under the guidance of the

24. González, "The Rule of Faith: The Early Church's Source of Unity and Diversity" (1998), 98.

25. Radner and Sumner (eds.), *The Rule of Faith* (1998).

26. Westra, "*Regula Fidei* and Other Creedal Formulations in the *Acts of Peter*" (1998).

Spirit. Upon this "common confession" is based the doctrinal unity of the church and through it the Scriptures are interpreted.[27]

Irenaeus, as the first author to make extensive use of the canon of truth, understandably is the object of many studies. Addressing a contemporary issue in the Anglican Church, R. L. R. Paice gave a thorough examination of Irenaeus's views on Scripture, the rule of truth, and episcopacy. Scripture was supreme for Irenaeus. The rule of truth is derived from Scripture and provides an unchanging and coherent system against which other systems are measured. Episcopal succession is not a source of doctrine but the means by which scriptural doctrine is handed on.[28]

Bryan M. Litfin studied Tertullian's use of the rule of faith for interpretation of Scripture in his work *Against Marcion*. Tertullian took the *regula* as the general interpretive device that provided the metanarrative—comparable to Irenaeus's *hypothesis* (the plot) of Scripture; that is, the framework of the biblical storyline—to which individual scriptural passages must conform (see our chapter 3). Tertullian saw the Bible story as presenting a cosmic Christology.[29]

Paul Hartog calls attention to the use of the rule of faith in patristic biblical exegesis. For Irenaeus, essential doctrines are set forth in Scripture (*Against Heresies* 2.27). The rule of faith was not a competitor with Scripture but provided the plot or hypothesis of the Scripture narrative. Tertullian called this central message the *ratio* of Scripture (*Prescription against Heretics* 9); the rule and Scripture

27. Henderson, "Irenaeus on the Rule of Faith" (2001).

28. Paice, "Irenaeus on the Authority of Scripture, the Rule of Truth, and Episcopacy" (2003).

29. Litfin, "Tertullian's Use of the *Regula Fidei* as an Interpretive Device in *Adversus Marcionem*" (2006).

belong together (*Prescription against Heretics* 19). Later Athanasius used the word *skopos* (goal) to describe the function of the rule in relation to Scripture (*Against the Arians* 3.27, 28, 35, 58). The rule of faith provides a narrative, or perhaps a metanarrative, so individual passages are to be approached in the light of the whole story. Since there is a unity in the narrative, Scripture interprets Scripture. This narrative is Christ-centered. The rule establishes a framework with boundaries for interpretation of Scripture. The worshipping community, created by the rule, is the proper context for an authoritative reading and full understanding of Scripture.[30]

Jonathan J. Armstrong's main concern is the relation of the rule of faith with the New Testament canon.[31] He provides a helpful survey of the history of scholarship on the rule of faith, from Theodor Zahn to Heinz Ohme,[32] from which we have drawn some of our own survey earlier in this chapter. From these earlier studies he notes among their conclusions that the rule cannot be identified with the baptismal confession and had an anti-heretical purpose. For Irenaeus, the rule of truth is the content of Scripture and served as a hermeneutical principle. Tertullian appears to equate the rule with Scripture in *Against Marcion* 3.17. Origen, it is claimed, used canon to refer to the Scriptures. Armstrong cites Augustine's statements on the authority of Scripture.

Wieslaw Davidowski summarized his doctoral dissertation in giving a thorough study of the use and function

30. Hartog, "The 'Rule of Faith' and Patristic Biblical Exegesis" (2007).

31. See note 5.

32. See earlier in this chapter on Zahn. Heinz Ohme (*Kanon Ekklesiastikos*, 1998) finds that for Irenaeus Scripture itself is the canon of truth (ibid., 68).

of the rule of faith in Augustine. In addition to *regula fidei* he surveyed seven other phrases parallel to but not identical in meaning to the rule of faith. Augustine's doctrine of illumination—ideas in the mind that are the effect of God communicating with the world—is a common denominator of his varied terminology. The *regula fidei* served as a vehicle for transmitting and communicating the faith. It had a normative function enabling one to distinguish between orthodox and heterodox opinions (*The Trinity* 2.10.7). It was one criterion for deciding canonicity (*On the Agreement of the Evangelists* 1.1.2). It was derived from Scripture, but Augustine also suggests that it had other sources (*City of God* 11.33).[33]

Alexander Y. Hwang, in the same volume with Armstrong's article, carries the study of the rule of faith to a later period than I cover. Prosper of Aquitaine represents the emerging Western tradition of a rule of faith determined by the Roman church. John Cassian and Vincent of Lérins maintained a view of the rule of faith in terms of tradition, but tradition for them consisted of the consensus of the church, that is what the church declared through ecumenical councils and the concordant opinions of the church fathers.[34]

Alistair Stewart, beginning with Irenaeus's information, looked at the role of the rule of faith in catechesis. *Against Heresies* 1.10.1 was a trinitarian statement followed by a christological supplement. Stewart argues that the catechetical process known to Irenaeus involved a "handing

33. Davidowski, "*Regula Fidei* in Augustine: Its Use and Function" (2004), especially 255–58, 297–98 for discussion relating to my comments. See my chapter two for the terminology employed by Augustine. We shall return to this work in chapter five.

34. Hwang, "Prosper, Cassian, and Vincent: The Rule of Faith in the Augustinian Controversy" (2010), 85.

on" to the candidate for baptism a trinitarian creedal formula (*Against Heresies* 1.9.4). At the declaration of assent to Christ (the *syntaxis*) there was a declaratory christological confession. He cites the evidence for a christological confession at baptism (Acts 8:37 in Codex D; Pseudo-Hippolytus, *Theophany*; *Apostolic Constitutions* 7.41.3; Chrysostom, *Catechetical Homilies* 2.20–21). He thinks it wrong that the earliest baptismal professions were interrogatory and trinitarian, a position that has led to misunderstanding Irenaeus.[35] His interpretation is in line with the position I take in chapter 5 that the rule of faith had to do with church's teaching and was separate in function from the baptismal confession.

Another work focusing on the rule and the interpretation of Scripture is by Zdravko Jovanovič, who deals with Irenaeus and the ecclesiological context of interpretation. He states erroneously, or perhaps loosely, that Irenaeus introduced *regula fidei* into theological discourse, for his usual wording was "rule of truth." The Gnostics' appeal to some Scriptures with their own interpretation necessitated Irenaeus's appeal to the rule. The church community is the primary *locus* of the authentic interpretation of Scripture. Irenaeus wanted to take theological discourse out of the sphere of speculation and put it in the context of the experience of the church. I would say rather that he sought to put it in the context of the plot of Scripture. As Jovanovič says, there is a close analogy between, if not identity of, the *regula* and the *hypothesis* (storyline) of Scripture, which is the background or structure of God's revelation. Interpretation belongs not just to the few, but to the whole community. Clear passages interpret the difficult ones. The *regula* was not a rival or surrogate for the Bible but a summary

35. Stewart, "'The Rule of Faith . . . which He Received through Baptism' (*Haer* 1.9.4)" (2012).

of the most important Christian doctrines, and thus could be used as a criterion for authentic interpretation. And the essence of the biblical narrative is christocentric.[36]

Tomas Bokedal[37] affirms that the defining genitive in rule of faith and rule of truth indicates that the faith or the truth itself is the rule or norm for Christian belief and practice. The Greek κανών (*kanōn*) had two basic meanings—straightness and measure. Its figurative uses included precision, representation, a limit (as a boundary), and, in the context of church conflict, a rule or norm. Irenaeus ("canon of truth"), Tertullian ("rule of faith"), and Clement of Alexandria ("ecclesiastical canon") traced the concept back to Christ and the apostles. He concentrates on Irenaeus' usage and concludes that, even if the immediate context for appeal to the *regula* was often apologetic, its features indicate a non-apologetic setting of its structure and traditional elements.

A recent study by Jobi Patteruparampil permits inclusion of the usage in Syriac of Ephrem. Finding the first context of the rule of faith in baptism (Irenaeus, *Against Heresies* 1.9.4), Patteruparampil finds it also in polemics against Gnostics, in catechesis, liturgy, and exorcism. The theological context in Ephrem the Syrian is the struggle against the outsiders (Manichaeans, Marcionites, Bardaisanites, and Jews) and insider adversaries, such as Sabellians and Arians. Against the heresies Ephrem proposes to uphold the unity of the Scriptures, to have a childlike faith, and to accept the limits of reason. His sermons and hymns on faith were directed against the intellectual leaders of the Arian party in the Syriac-speaking church. The trinitarian formula at baptism was basic: "On three names hangs our

36. Jovanovič, "St. Irenaeus, *Regula Fidei* and the Ecclesiological Context of Interpretation" (2013).

37. Bokedal, "The Rule of Faith: Tracing Its Origins" (2013).

baptism; by three mysteries has our faith been victorious" (*Hymns on Faith* 13.5). A representative quotation is, "You have heard of the Father, Son, and Holy Spirit, so conclude from the names the true reality of persons" (*Sermons on Faith* IV, 45).[38] Patteruparampil uses "rule of faith" as equal to the creed. That usage brings us full circle around the intervening studies that distinguished them back to where modern studies began.

We may bring our survey to a conclusion at the present with an examination of the revised doctoral dissertation by Jonathan J. Armstrong on Eusebius of Caesarea. Armstrong uses "rule of faith" not for a precisely worded set of teachings, but for the apostolic deposit of faith. Eusebius was influenced by Irenaeus on the fourfold Gospel canon and by Origen on the rest of the New Testament, thus making Origen a progenitor of the New Testament canon. Eusebius derived from the former the importance of apostolicity, and from the latter the importance of catholicity (usage current in the churches) for determining canonicity. The rule of faith as the body of orthodox doctrine served for Eusebius as the criterion of apostolicity and of catholicity and thus was a criterion of canonicity.[39]

These studies present us with the issues surrounding the study of the rule of faith in the early church and prepare for a consideration of the functions it had and in the light of these what its contemporary relevance might be.

---

38. Patteruparampil, "*Regula Fidei* in Ephrem's *Hymni de Fide* LXVII and in *Sermones de Fide* IV" (2013), 187, 190.

39. Armstrong, *The Role of the Rule of Faith in the Formation of the New Testament Canon according to Eusebius of Caesarea* (2014).

Discussion Questions

1. What studies of the Rule of Faith seem most compelling to you?

2. What are indications of considerable scholarly interest in the Rule of Faith?

3. Why do you suppose there is not an extended, comprehensive study of the Rule of Faith?

Functions of the Rule of Faith

Much of the study of the rule of faith concerns its relationship to a creed, particularly the baptismal confession of faith, known as the symbol, that became the Apostles Creed.[1] Some saw the creed as coming first and the rule of faith as derived from it and something of a commentary on it. Others reversed the relation and studied the various statements of the rule as leading to a condensed formulation in the finished baptismal confession. It is the contention of this study that these approaches misunderstand the relation of the rule of faith and the creed. Their history represents parallel developments. The rule of faith summarized the preaching and teaching of the evangelists and teachers in the church, that is, the objective faith of the church; and the baptismal confession was the faith professed by candidates for baptism, which was the subjective acceptance of, and identification with, the gospel that

1. See chapter four for the history of scholarship on the rule of faith.

had been taught. Both were initially variable in wording, and this remained true for the rule of faith. Each evangelist and teacher had his own way of presenting the message of salvation in Christ, according to his understandings and concerns, the needs of the hearers, and the circumstances of the time. The baptismal creed as a liturgically repeated formula by all candidates for baptism tended toward—and eventually received—a fixity, or relative fixity, of wording. The content of the rule of faith and the symbol was similar, and this circumstance led to them being studied in relation to each other. What was preached was what was confessed, and one confessed faith in what had been taught. However, the rule of faith and the creed had *different functions*, and these functions influenced their wording and development. Our concern here is the functions of the rule of faith.

Preaching and Teaching

The introduction to chapter three noted the connection of the rule of faith to the preaching of the church, going back to accounts in the New Testament of apostolic preaching. Early Christian writers consistently described the rule of faith/canon of truth as *what* was preached and taught. It represented the *content* of the proclamation of the gospel and the instruction given to inquirers and potential converts.[2] We note here some of the early statements to this effect.

Irenaeus prefaced his account of the faith by saying it was the "truth proclaimed by the church" (*Against Heresies* 1.9.5). After a trinitarian statement of the "one and same faith" delivered by the apostles (quoted in chapter

2. Quasten, "Regula fidei," 1103, noted that the rule of faith was identical with neither the Holy Scripture nor the oral tradition but with the apostolic *kerygma* that underlies both.

3), Irenaeus says this is "the firm and true preaching of the church, according to which the one and same way of salvation is shown in the whole world. . . . For the church everywhere preaches the truth" (*Against Heresies* 5.20.1).[3] In his *Demonstration of the Apostolic Preaching* he summarized the contents as "the preaching of the truth" (*Demonstration* 98). Clement of Alexandria identified the rule with the "tradition of the blessed teaching from the apostles" (*Miscellanies* 1.1.15.2). Tertullian argued that the rule was known from the fact that Christ sent the apostles to preach, and what they preached is proved by the churches they founded (*Prescription against Heretics* 21); the apostles made known and proclaimed "the whole system of the rule" (*Prescription against Heretics* 27.1). Origen introduced his listing of essential Christian doctrines by saying, "The holy apostles, when preaching the faith of Christ," delivered in plain terms to believers the necessary doctrines to be believed (*On First Principles* preface 3).

The rule of faith, therefore, represents the preaching of the church. It summarizes and outlines the (objective) faith, the truth of God's plan and the gospel of Christ. The settings in which this proclamation and this teaching might be given were, of course, varied:

- preaching in the assembly of the church (Melito, *On the Pascha*);

- street corner and other public preaching, where this was possible (implicit in Lucian, *On the Death of Peregrinus* 11–16);

3. The passage includes the assertion that the church possesses the sure tradition of the apostles and shows that the faith is one and the same: receiving one and the same God the Father, the same dispensation regarding the incarnation of the Son of God, the same gift of the Spirit, the same commandments, the same form of ecclesiastical constitution, and expecting the same advent of the Lord and same salvation of soul and body.

- testifying before authorities in trials (martyr literature such as *Acts of Justin* 5–7; *Martyrdom of Apollonius* 8; 15; 36–37);

- private conversations with family, friends, and acquaintances, or with fellow-workers (cf. Celsus in Origen, *Against Celsus* 3.55);

- formulas used in exorcism (Justin, 2 *Apology* 6; *Dialogue with Trypho* 85.2).

Instruction of New Converts

A particular form of the use of the rule of faith in teaching was the instruction of new converts immediately before and immediately after baptism. This teaching is known as catechesis.

We discussed in chapter four the thesis of L. W. Countryman that the rule of faith for Tertullian was catechetical instruction. This is a plausible proposal. Tertullian expected all Christians to be familiar with the rule of faith. His statements of what was contained in the rule have a similar content. However, their wording is different; the items have a different order; and not all have the same items included. Hence, the rule could not have been something recited in a liturgical setting. The other likely context in which all could have become familiar with the contents of the rule would have been preaching in church or more specifically in instruction in connection with baptism. Indeed, Irenaeus says, as we noted in chapter 2, that a person "received the rule of truth through baptism" (*Against Heresies* 1.9.4). This statement is commonly taken to refer to a formula of faith delivered to the candidate for him or her to confess. More likely, it refers to the instruction that accompanied the preparation for baptism. This rule of truth summarized "the faith that the church, although scattered to the ends of the earth, received from the apostles and their disciples" (*Against Heresies* 1.10.4), a statement more aptly describing the preaching of the gospel than a confessional formula.

Irenaeus's *Demonstration of the Apostolic Preaching* may be described as a commentary on or fuller communication of the rule of faith (see chapter 3). In this work, according to the Armenian translation, Irenaeus used the term "rule of faith" (*Demonstration* 6) instead of his favorite designation "rule of truth." The *Demonstration* is sometimes taken as having an apologetic or polemical purpose, because of the anti-heretical content.[4] Irenaeus, preoccupied with the Gnostic threat, let no opportunity pass to make a thrust against heretical teaching. The main content and purpose of the *Demonstration*, however, seems to be elsewhere. The bulk of the treatise is in two blocks: a literal history of the mighty acts of God the Father beginning with the creation, continuing the biblical story through the coming of Christ, and concluding with the sending of the apostles and the general resurrection (8–42a); then the telling of the story of Jesus from the prophecies fulfilled by him—his preexistence, his divine nature, his virgin birth, his miracles, his passion, his resurrection, and his calling of a new people through the apostles (42b–97). The prophecies are presented not so much as a proof as an exposition about Christ. I have earlier argued that the treatise accords better with what we know about early catechetical instruction.[5] This purpose fits the presentation of doctrine and morals into a historical framework. Irenaeus's summary of the work near the end (98) presents a sequence of preaching, salvation, and way of life; makes reference to what the church handed

4. As by Smith, *St. Irenaeus Proof of the Apostolic Preaching.*

5. Everett Feguson, "Irenaeus's Proof of the Apostolic Preaching and Early Catechetical Instruction."

down to its members; and insisted on maintaining a good moral life. These were motifs of the catechetical process.[6] It may be that "those who wish to hear" mentioned at the beginning of the treatise (1) are the "hearers," a term for the catechumens. I proposed that the Marcianus to whom the treatise is addressed may have been a teacher and this work a manual to guide him in his instruction of new converts.

If R. P. C. Hanson is correct, the similar formulations of the rule of faith by Victorinus (bishop of Pettau in the latter half of the third century) and Patrick (missionary bishop to Ireland in the fifth century) is accounted for by the adoption in Patrick's homeland of Britain in the fourth century of Victorinus's formulation as a basis of catechetical instruction. Their similar statements are not creeds but rules of faith. Patrick passed on a traditional formula that was regularly handed on to neophytes. Both Victorinus and Patrick used the unusual phrase *mensurius fidei* ("measure/limit/full extent of faith") for their formulations (Victorinus, *Commentary on the Apocalypse* 11; Patrick, *Confession* 4).[7]

Refutation of Heresy

Scholarship has stressed the anti-heretical use of the rule of faith. This function of the rule of faith is obvious and explicit in Irenaeus and Tertullian. Irenaeus's treatise *Against Heresies* begins its "Exposition and Overthrow of the Gnosis Falsely So-Called" by setting forth the system of Ptolemy, a follower of Valentinus (1–8), followed by the refutation, which is introduced by a statement of the "canon of truth" (1.9.4—1.10.2). From this platform Irenaeus

---

6. Turck, *Évangelisaton et catéchèse aux deux premiers siècles.*

7. Hanson, "The Rule of Faith of Victorinus and of Patrick."

launches his refutation of the interpretations advanced by heretics. Thomas C. K. Ferguson concludes that Irenaeus formulated the rule of truth by appropriation of terms and concepts found in his descriptions of Gnosticism.[8]

Two of Tertullian's statements of the rule of faith occur in treatises with an avowedly anti-heretical purpose: *On the Prescription of Heretics* (13) presented as a legal argument denying those outside the catholic church the right to appeal to Scriptures, which are not theirs, and *Against Praxeas* (2), a doctrinal treatise against the Modalist interpretation that made the Father and the Son one person instead of two. *On the Veiling of Virgins* has a different setting, for it begins by setting up the contrast between the rule of faith, which is unchangeable, and practical disciplinary matters, which are subject to change. *On the Prescription of Heretics* begins with what Tertullian calls his preamble, namely general reflections on the nature of heresies—the necessity of their existence, their appeal to human weakness, biblical warnings against them, their origin in pagan philosophy, and the need to cease searching after finding divine knowledge. Tertullian then begins the transition to his argument that the Scriptures belong only to those to whom they were given, that is catholic Christians, by recounting the rule of faith. Matters of searching, inquiry, and curiosity must not transgress the rule of faith.

Tertullian objected to Praxeas (either a proper name or a characterization of the opponent as a "Busybody") on the grounds that the latter made God the Father to have suffered on the cross (Patipassianism) and that he, unlike Tertullian, rejected the New Prophecy associated with Montanus. Tertullian set forth the rule of faith straightaway as having come down from the beginning of the gospel,

8. Thomas C. K. Ferguson, "The Rule of Truth and Irenaean Rhetoric in Book 1 of *Against Heresies*," 361, 375.

long before Praxeas's time. This rule of faith distributed the unity of the one God into a Trinity of Father, Son, and Holy Spirit. The rest of the treatise aimed to show that, although these were three in number, they were not divided.

Noetus was another teacher of the Modalist, or Patripassian, interpretation of the Father and the Son. The presbyters at Smyrna who condemned him and Hippolytus reasoned from statements characteristic of the rule of faith in refuting him.

Clement of Alexandria too used the rule as an anti-heretical instrument, although not as explicitly or elaborately as Irenaeus and Tertullian. After referring to the "rule of truth," Clement referred to one "who has ceased to be a person of God and to remain faithful to the Lord, spurning the ecclesiastical tradition and darting after the opinions of human heresies." This person on hearing the Scriptures may return to the truth, "For we have the source of our teaching the Lord through the prophets, and the gospel, and the blessed apostles" (*Miscellanies* 7.16.95).

The synod of church leaders in Antioch in the mid-third century that condemned the teaching of Paul of Samosata described him as "having departed from the rule [*kanōn*] and turned aside to fraudulent and spurious doctrines" (Eusebius, *Church History* 7.30.6).

Origen's *Commentary on Matthew* 24:20–28, preserved mainly in Latin (and so not necessarily reflecting Origen's own terminology), referred to the Law, Prophets, and apostles as authority, spoke of "the canonical Scriptures in which every Christian believes and consents, and identifies a phrase of Scripture as "word of truth" (series 46). There follows an anti-heretical thrust: "We ought not to believe those things nor to leave the first and ecclesiastical tradition nor believe any thing other than what was delivered to us by the succession of the church of God." A brief quotation of the Greek says, "The one outside the faith and the canon of the church and of the Scripture." The Latin adds, "Wanting to show those words which are in every respect outside Scripture, he says, 'If they say to you, "Behold he is in solitude," do not go out' [Matt 24:26] from the rule of faith" (series 46).

Many features of the rule of faith lent themselves well to a refutation of the false teachings threatening the church in the second and third centuries. These included the affirmation that the one God the Father was the Creator of all that is, that Jesus Christ was the Son of God, fully God and fully human, and that this Christ was prophesied by the Holy Spirit. These points responded to the Gnostic demotion of the Creator God (the Demiurge) to a lesser status than the supreme Father and Marcion's distinction of two gods, the Old Testament Creator God of justice and the New Testament's merciful Father of Jesus Christ. The statements about Christ related him to the creation and the Creator God and affirmed his historical connection with the Old Testament Scriptures, but they particularly emphasized his full humanity involved in birth from a virgin, crucifixion under Pilate, and bodily resurrection. The work of the Holy Spirit most consistently mention was the inspiration of the prophets, so again drawing the connection of Christ with Israel and Israel's Scriptures.

The function of the rule in refuting false teaching and its usefulness for this purpose are obvious. The question, remains, however: Was this the *original* purpose of the rule of faith? Was it constructed for an anti-heretical argument? or did it exist *prior* to its being used for this purpose? The latter seems to be the case, as many scholars recognize. There are features of the rule of faith that do not have a specifically anti-heretical thrust, even after allowance is made for the selective nature of each author's choice of what to include and how to word the selection. The emphasis on the second coming, judgment, and righteous living might have some relevance to the struggle with heresy but seem to be included to present a comprehensive scheme of the divine plan. Some incidentals included in some of the statements seem unnecessary for refuting heresy, such as naming Mary and Pilate and reference to the resurrection "on the third day" and to the session on the "right hand" of the Father. These appear to be points derived from the original formulations of the message.

The perspective adopted in this volume is that the rule of faith belongs in continuity with early summaries of the apostolic preaching and teaching. As such it could be used as a standard against which to judge later teaching, and it was indeed effective for this purpose. The essential content of the rule of faith existed *before* its anti-heretical use, however much specific wordings of the rule may have been adapted to later circumstances.

Interpretation of Scripture

Several passages relate the rule of faith to Scripture. For Irenaeus, the contents of the rule of truth were set forth in Scripture (*Against Heresies* 2.27.1); God's words are the rule of truth (4.35.4). Some statements seem to identify Scripture itself as the rule of faith. Tertullian does so in one statement (*Against Marcion* 3.17.5). Origen had some of the strongest statements about the authority of Scripture, and he occasionally related it to the rule: note, for instance, the way in which "rule of Scripture" and "rule of Christian truth" are used as parallel expressions (*On First Principles* 3.3.4). One passage identifies an allusion to Scripture as the "canon of the church" (*Homilies on Jeremiah* 5.14.1); similarly Origen refers to ideas "outside the faith and canon of the church and Scripture" (*Commentary on Matthew* on Matt 22:34—27:63). More likely than simply identifying Scripture as the rule of faith, these authors were expressing the idea that *the rule of faith and Scripture testify to the same truth*. Although the rule of faith was distinct from Scripture, it was not set over against Scripture as a separate source of authority.

The rule of faith provided a framework for the interpretation of Scripture. For Irenaeus the term *hypothesis* (ὑπόθεσις—*Against Heresies* 1.9.4) for the "plotline" or "fundamental outline" of Scripture seems to be equivalent to the "canon of truth." Clement of Alexandria expressly says that the Scriptures are to be explained according to the rule of truth (*Miscellanies* 6.15.124.5). For him and for others an important principle of interpretation was the ecclesiastical rule of the harmony of the Law and Prophets with the new covenant of Christ (*Miscellanies* 6.15.125.3).

The positive side of the role of the rule of faith in interpreting Scripture was to understand difficult passages according to what was set forth in the rule. The "apprehension and comprehension of the truth through the truth" (*Miscellanies* 5.1.1.4) was another way of saying to interpret Scripture by Scripture. Augustine in discussing the interpretation of Scripture said that if a passage is uncertain, "let the reader consult the rule of faith that is gathered from the plain passages of Scripture and from the authority of the church," and he gives examples. Furthermore, he suggested that ambiguity is cleared up by the rule of faith or by the context of the passage (*On Christian Doctrine* 3.2.2 and 5).

The negative function of the rule of faith in interpretation was to rule out erroneous and unacceptable readings of Scripture ("what does not impair the rule of faith"—Tertullian, *Prescription against Heretics* 12.5). It was as true for interpreting the Bible as for formulating theological ideas that, as Clement of Alexandria stated, "It is proper for us in no way to transgress the ecclesiastical rule" (*Miscellanies* 7.15.90.5).

Authors allowed multiple interpretations provided they did not transgress the boundaries set by the rule of faith. Origen thus defended his theological speculations on the grounds that they were not going against the teachings clearly and generally believed by Christians.

Augustine allowed that a text may have more than one meaning, and he referred to Ambrose's *Commentary on Luke* where Ambrose comments "in different ways which do not depart from the rule of faith" (Augustine, *Against Julian* 2.5.10). Augustine followed the same principle. In interpreting Ephesians 3:18–19, he referred to what "does not conflict with the rule of faith" (*Letter* 147.14.34). In dealing with the question of why the Holy Spirit was given twice, (John 20:22; Acts 2:4) Augustine observed that some interpreters said one thing and some another but none should go against the standard of truth (*Sermon* 265.9). The principle applied to theology as well as exegesis, for he advised, "If you have come to some understanding that does not differ from the rule of the catholic faith," add to the building, but do not forsake the foundation (*Tractates on John* 98.7).

One could also make inferences from the contents of the rule: "Anyone faithfully considering the rule of faith cannot deny that the Son of God was predestined" (*Tractates on John* 105.8).

Augustine used the rule of faith as an interpretive devise in his *On Christian Doctrine*. His uses of the rule in exegesis may be grouped in three categories:

- as a summary of the church's interpretation,

- as a criterion of theological judgments,

- and as an orthodox boundary line within which there

is exegetical flexibility.[9]

Summary from Augustine

Augustine's extensive writings provide a summary of the diverse functions served by the rule of faith in early Christian authors.

Interpreting the Scriptures

The preceding paragraphs show Augustine's understanding of the role of the rule of faith in interpreting Scripture. It provided a standard for understanding the Bible and its teaching. He spoke of the practice of offering the sacrifice of the Eucharist for the souls of the unbaptized as "a novel idea, foreign the church's discipline and the rule of faith" (*Nature and Origin of the Soul* 2.11.15). The rule of faith regulates interpretation (*On Eighty-Three Varied Questions* 69.1). One should "approve what should be approved and reject what should be rejected in accordance with the rule of faith" (*Nature and Origin of the Soul* 2.17.23). Augustine says that the interpreter should seek the meaning intended by the biblical author; if this is not evident, the context should guide; and an interpretation should be adopted that agrees with the faith, for any meaning that does not depart from pious belief is acceptable (*On the Literal Interpretation of Genesis* 1). He several times asserts the principle "Whatever interpretation emerges, it must conform to the rule of faith" (*Explanations of the Psalms* 74.12); compare, "No matter which of the [interpretations] is preferred none of them transgresses the rule of faith" (*Explanations of the*

9. Litfin, "The Rule of Faith in Augustine," 89–90.

Psalms 9.6). The rule of faith was particularly helpful where passages appeared contradictory (*The Trinity* 2.10.7).

Resisting Heresy

Augustine joined with his predecessors in employing an anti-heretical function for the rule of faith. He says that writers of apocryphal gospels "introduced into their writings certain items that are condemned by the catholic and apostolic rule of faith and by sound doctrine" (*Agreement of the Evangelists* 1.1.2). One should "approve what should be approved and reject what should be rejected in accordance with the rule of faith" (*Nature and Origin of the Soul* 2.17.23), specifying the rejection and avoidance of heterodox opinions (*On the Literal Interpretation of Genesis* 12.14). One is not to make statements that depart from the rule of faith (*On the Merits and Forgiveness of Sins* 2.27.43). Inadequate understandings by those in the church who lacked spiritual maturity could be overlooked if they held to the unity of the church: since in order not to withdraw from the unity of the church, "they persistently hold in the church the rule of faith common to the least and to the greater ones," as they make progress in spirituality (*Letter* 187.29). The principle went further, for anything faultily uttered in prayer over the water of baptism contrary to the rule of faith was overridden by one's right intentions and the power of the fixed words of the gospel [that is, the baptismal formula] (*On Baptism* 6.25.47).

A Norm for Doctrine

The rule of faith constituted the fixed norm of Christian doctrine (cf. *Sermon* 362.7). The truths of the faith are stated in the rule (*Letter* 193.4.11). The rule is that "by which we are Christians" (*On the Grace of Christ and Original Sin* 2.29.34). In keeping with his identification of the rule of faith with the creed, Augustine reasoned that if the Holy Spirit were a creature, "he would not be placed in the rule of faith before the church" (*Enchiridion* 15.56).

Faith Seeking Understanding

Wieslaw Davidowski's thorough examination of Augustine's usage of the rule of faith and related terms summarized these functions and added one more with reference to Augustine. He identified four linguistic contexts in which this terminology appears: (1) The rule of faith embraced the contents of the Christian faith as handed on from the apostles and received in baptism. It gave stability and permanence. (2) The rule of faith had an apologetic function of discerning what belongs to the orthodox faith. It established sound doctrine for the church and right belief for its members. (3) The rule of faith had an exegetical function as a criterion for interpretation. It was a hermeneutical tool for theological inquiry. (4) The rule of faith provided an epistemological context for reason seeking to understand what is believed (*Sermon* 213.12, the rule guides the mind in understanding what is to be believed). On this level it was a guide for intellectual activity.[10]

For all the authors we may say that the rule of faith, by testifying to God's salvation in Christ, pointed to authentic Christian identity.

10. Davidowski, "*Regula Fidei* in Augustine," 259–60, 296.

Discussion Questions

1. Why do you suppose there is not an extended, comprehensive study of the Rule of Faith?

2. Suggest other functions the Rule of Faith might serve today?

3. Evaluate the Rule of Faith as a guide to interpreting Scripture.

4. What gives Christians their identity? What core of beliefs establish this identity?

SIX

Relevance for Today of the Rule of Faith

Insofar as the formulations of the rule of faith were re-statements of the apostolic preaching, the rule of faith is as relevant today as the gospel. Despite the scientific, technological, economic, and medical advances, the human condition remains essentially the same. The nature of God, Christ, and the Holy Spirit remain the same. The facts of what God has done in Christ remain the same and still need to be proclaimed. Underlying human nature remains the same. Human sins may seem more sophisticated and their justifications may seem more acceptable, but their effects on human society remain as devastating as ever. Therefore, the gospel, as God's answer to the human condition, continues to be deeply relevant. And the rule of faith as a summary of the basic facts of the gospel shares that relevance. There are a number of aspects of the contemporary value of the "canon of truth" that are worth spelling out as we conclude.

A Succinct Statement of Core Doctrine

For inquirers, new converts, and the congregation

Churches, especially non-creedal churches, but others as well, often need succinct statements of their basic doctrines—in addressing inquirers or visitors, in instructing new converts, or in clarifying their core beliefs to Christians who seek to identify with them. The rule of faith can serve these purposes well. It can explain to newcomers or visitors what the congregation believes. In the conversion process it lays out what is necessary to accept. For the further instruction on new converts the rule of faith promotes the learning of who we are as the people of God. In the continuing public proclamation of the church, a statement of the rule of faith focuses the message, keeping it biblical. For either expanding or limiting the fellowship of a congregation, the rule of faith clarifies what can and cannot be accepted. It limits what is not open for discussion or reinterpretation, but gives freedom to change other things.

For leaders

For those who would be leaders in a congregation, the rule of faith indicates what must be embraced, taught, and handed on. Those individuals who think they "know" more than others must not forget this limitation. The leaders in a congregation, grounded in the contents of the rule of faith, can more readily combat false teaching, for what is easier to understand is easier to affirm. The rule of faith was a simple distillation of the essential Christian message. Such a brief and clear statement invites acceptance and faith. Furthermore, it sustains unity in diversity and disagreement.

The confession that Jesus is Lord (Rom 10:9) involves accepting the facts about him and following his teachings. It thus becomes the standard for initiation into the fellowship of believers and the guide for conduct toward other professing Christians.

Creedal statements, in contrast, typically demand acceptance of something outside of Scripture and possibly beyond the teaching of the apostles. Creeds began as baptismal confessions of faith in the early centuries. By the fourth century they became increasingly tests of fellowship (note the anathemas attached to the original creed adopted at Nicaea in 325). Creeds in this line of development by their nature and very formulation create division by marking off those who do not accept the creed's affirmations. As a consequence many persons came to identify (and still do) their creed as their "rule of faith." The rule of faith, in its original functions, as a more fluid summary of Scripture, tends more to encourage the broader unity that the creeds hoped to create.

Discerning the Centre from the Periphery in Christian Doctrine

The rule of faith is relevant as a reminder of the *core doctrines* of Christianity. Unlike some of the later creeds, the rule of faith does not seek to give a philosophical or advanced theological explanation of the faith. Rather it proclaims the content of the faith. It does not go into detail on many important doctrinal points. These other doctrinal points are important for theological reflection. The basis for these further reflections, however, remains the essential facts that lie at the heart of Christian faith. Origen's distinction between those items certainly believed by all Christians and those topics open for discussion retains its usefulness, even if one might draw the line elsewhere than Origen did. From the Christian viewpoint, there are some things that are non-negotiable. To borrow Origen's wording, the apostles delivered the necessary doctrines in "the plainest terms to all believers" (*On First Principles* preface, quoted in chapter one). The basic facts of the gospel are simple and must be kept simple. The rule of faith does this. However much Christians may differ on many topics, there are some items on which they are united in their teaching. The rule helps the church to discern which topics those should be.

Testing Teachings

The core doctrines of the Christian faith serve as a touchstone for testing other ideas. The early church confronted heretical versions of the Christian faith, and orthodox believers countered these ideas by appealing to the rule of faith. It can serve the same function today. There are many competing worldviews in the contemporary world. Some are completely antithetical to historic Christianity; others have a tinge of Christian teaching about them. The rule should continue to play its role as a measure by which all such teachings can be tested. Many, for instance, find a place for Jesus and some of his ethical teachings in their systems of thought, but this is not enough to make them "Christian" according to the historical meaning of that name, according the measure of the rule of faith.

Keeping the Focus on Christ and His Story

The relevance of the rule of faith comes especially from the fact that it centers on Jesus Christ. It relates Jesus to God the Father as his Son and to the Holy Spirit as the divine gift to the church. But above all else, the rule of faith proclaims Christ as the Eternal Son of the Father, as the Word who became flesh through birth from the virgin Mary, who experienced fully human life, was crucified under Pontius Pilate for the sins of humanity, was raised from the dead, and is coming again as judge of the living and the dead. The facts about Jesus were central to Christian preaching and Christian faith from the beginning. This centrality of Christ and the affirmations about him distinguish Christianity from the Judaism out of which it arose, from Islam, which came later, and from other religions that do not have the same historical basis and same kind of inspired Scriptures as these Abrahamic faiths. It is good for Christians to emphasize this commonality in their faith, especially when occasions arise where their differences are at the forefront.

The vision of God presented in the story of the incarnation represents a radical Christian alternative to the portrayal of the Deity in, for instance, Islam, especially in its radical expressions. The God who became man in the person of Jesus Christ, and set aside his own rights out of love for others, is a different kind of God from the God worshipped in Islam. The incarnation and Christ's atoning death mark Christian faith off from competing world religions.

The central emphasis on Jesus Christ includes how he relates to the one God, Creator of heaven and earth, as his eternal Word and Son, and how he was prophesied in the Hebrew Scriptures. The emphasis in the early preaching on the fulfillment of the Old Testament demonstrates God's trustworthiness and enables us to trust in him. Worship of Christ as Lord and Savior did not compromise the explicit affirmation of monotheism. This one Lord Jesus Christ continues to relate to the ongoing life of the church through his gift of the Holy Spirit. The "one and only God" counters "new age" thought that offers a different view of the divine and of human spirituality. This emphasis on the one God stands against putting one's ego in the forefront and against a self-centeredness in religious matters.

Guiding Biblical Interpretation

The rule of faith, furthermore, will set parameters around one's interpretation of Scripture. It does not necessarily decide the correct meaning of a difficult passage of Scripture, but it does rule out obviously incorrect meanings. As some early writers pointed out, various interpretations of a passage may be acceptable if they do not transgress the fundamentals of the faith. The rule of faith as a standard for interpretation prevents a heretical or an idiosyncratic reading of the Bible. It will point one to the main themes of Scripture, of which it provides a summary. The rule of faith, therefore, is relevant as calling attention to the main points of God's revelation in Scripture.

The rule of faith gives the big picture, the larger doctrinal and historical framework of the biblical revelation. The rule of faith reminds us to take the whole of Scripture, not a part of it or to set one part over against the rest, and to seek the underlying harmony. It affirms the unity of the Old and New Testaments.

Scripture is not "flat"; not all of it is of equal importance (cf. Matt 22:36–40 and 1 Cor 15:1–9). The rule of faith summarizes the most important facts of the gospel. Further exploration of theological, sociological, and psychological aspects of faith have value, if the first principles are not obscured.

Other Benefits of the Rule of Faith

The focus on the Creator-creation relation

Another important aspect of the rule is that the God who is worshipped is the *Creator* God. The doctrine of God as Creator provides the basis for a Christian approach to scientific and environmental issues. Attitudes toward nature and natural resources will be shaped by the recognition of the Creator.

The focus on the historical grounding of Christian faith

The rule of faith is relevant as a reminder of the historical grounding of the Christian faith. Jesus Christ lived a fully human life. He called the apostles to preach the gospel and set up the church. As time has passed, the rule of faith reminds us that however distant these events may seem, they did occur. This historical basis of Christianity resists the tendency to make up one's own version of Christianity.

*The reminder of coming judgment
and hope for resurrection*

This Jesus is proclaimed as the one who is coming again as judge. Recognition of judgment informs personal attitudes and conduct. By its reminder of accountability to the Eternal Judge, the rule of faith sets a boundary against making up one's own version of Christianity. This aspect of the rule of faith, furthermore, is a necessary check on the power and influence of an institutional church and church leaders.

The promise that Christ on his return will raise the dead provides hope to believers. That Jesus is Lord of the living and the dead is important for the pastoral care of the dying and the bereaved. The church— its members and ministers, draws its confidence in the face of death from the belief in resurrection testified to in the rule.

In view of these considerations it would be well for Christians to include the rule of faith in their theological studies and let it guide their thinking about the nature of Christianity.

Discussion Questions

1. Do you agree or disagree that the Rule of Faith has relevance for churches today? Give reasons for your answer.

2. Does the Rule of Faith have potential value for promoting unity among churches?

3. If churches were to include a study of the Rule of Faith in their curriculum of Bible study, what effects would this have?

Bibliography

Ammundsen, Valdemar. "The Rule of Truth in Irenaeus." *Journal of Theological Studies* 13 (1912) 574–80.

Armstrong, Jonathan J. "From the κανὼν τῆς ἀληθείας to the κανὼν τῶν γραφῶν: The Rule of Faith and the New Testament Canon." In *Tradition and the Rule of Faith in the Early Church: Essays in Honor of Joseph T. Lienhard, S.J*, edited by Ronnie J. Rombs and Alexander Y. Hwang, 30–47. Washington, DC: The Catholic University of America Press, 2010.

———. *The Role of the Rule of Faith in the Formation of the New Testament Canon according to Eusebius of Caesarea.* Lewiston, NY: Mellen, 2014.

Bardy, Gustav. "La Règle de Foi d'Origéne," *Recherches de Science Religieuse* 9 (1919) 162–96.

Blowers, Paul M. "The *Regula Fidei* and the Narrative Character of Early Christian Faith." *Pro Ecclesia* 6 (1997) 199–228.

Bokedal, Tomas. "The Rule of Faith: Tracing Its Origins," *Journal of Theological Interpretation* 7 (2013) 238–51.

Butterworth, G. W., trans. *Origen on First Principles.* London: SPCK, 1936.

Caspari, C. P. *Alte und neue Quellen zur Geschichte des Taufsymbols und der Glaubensregel.* Christiania, Denmark: Malling, 1879.

———. *Ungedruckte, unbeachtete und wenig beachtete Quellen zur Geschichte des Taufsymbols und der Glaubensregel.* 3 vols. Christiania: Malling, 1866, 1869, 1875.

Coan, Alphonse John. *The Rule of Faith in the Ecclesiastical Writings of the First Two Centuries: An Historico-Apologetical Investigation.* Washington, DC: Catholic University of America Press, 1924.

Countryman, L. W. "Tertullian and the Regula Fidei." *Second Century* 2 (1982) 208–27.

Bibliography

Davidowski, Wieslaw. "*Regula Fidei* in Augustine: Its Use and Function." *Augustinian Studies* 35 (2004) 253–99.

Dodd, C. H. *The Apostolic Preaching and Its Developments.* London: Hodder and Stoughton, 1963.

Farmer, William R. "Galatians and the Second-Century Development of the *Regula Fidei*." *The Second Century* 4 (1984) 143–70.

Ferguson, Everett. "Irenaeus's Proof of the Apostolic Preaching and Early Catechetical Instruction." *Studia Patristica* 18 (1989) 119–40; reprinted in Everett Ferguson, *The Early Church at Work and Worship*, Vol. 2: *Catechesis, Baptism, Eschatology, and Martyrdom*, 1–17. Eugene, OR: Cascade, 2014.

———. "Origen's Demonology." In *Johannine Studies: Essays in Honor of Frank Pack*, edited by James E. Priest, 54–66. Malibu, CA: Pepperdine University Press, 1989. Reprinted in Everett Fergusson, *The Early Church and Today*, vol. 1, 193–209. Abilene, TX: Abilene Christian University Press, 2012.

Ferguson, Thomas C. K. "The Rule of Truth and Irenaean Rhetoric in Book 1 of *Against Heresies*." *Vigiliae Christianae* 55 (2001) 356–75.

González, Catherine. "The Rule of Faith: The Early Church's Source of Unity and Diversity." In *Many Voices, One God: Being Faithful in a Pluralistic World: In Honor of Shirley C. Guthrie*, edited by W. Brueggemann and G. W. Stroup, 95–106. Louisville, KY: Westminster/John Knox, 1998.

Grech, Prosper S. "The *Regula Fidei* as a Hermeneutical Principle in Patristic Exegesis." In *The Interpretation of the Bible: The International Symposium in Slovenia*, edited by Jože Krašovec, 589–601. Journal for the Study of the Old Testament Supplement 289. Sheffield, UK: Sheffield Academic Press, 1998.

Hägglund, Bengt. "Die Bedeutung der 'regula fidei' als Grundlage theologischer Aussagen." *Studia Theologica* 12 (1958) 1–44.

Hahn, August. *Bibliothek der Symbole und Glaubensregeln der alten Kirche.* Breslau, Poland: Morgenstern, 1897.

Hanson, R. P. C. *Origen's Doctrine of Tradition.* London: SPCK, 1954.

———. "The Rule of Faith of Victorinus and of Patrick." In *Latin Script and Letters A.D. 400–900*, edited by J. J. O'Meara and Bernd Naumann, 25–36. Leiden: Brill, 1976.

Harnack, Adolf. *History of Dogma.* Translated from the 3rd German edition by Neil Buchanan. 7 vols. London: Constable and Company, 1900.

Hartog, Paul. "The 'Rule of Faith' and Patristic Biblical Exegesis." *Trinity Journal* 28 (2007) 65–86.

Henderson, David. "Irenaeus on the Rule of Faith." In *Reading the Bible in Faith: Theological Voices from the Pastorate*, edited by William H. Lazareth, 114–18. Grand Rapids: Eerdmans, 2001.

Hill, Edmund, translator. *Sermons III/6 on the Liturgical Seasons*. The Works of Saint Augustine: A Translation for the 21st Century. New Rochelle, NY: New City Press, 1993.

Hwang, Alexander. "Prosper, Cassian, and Vincent: The Rule of Faith in the Augustinian Controversy." In *Tradition and the Rule of Faith in the Early Church: Essays in Honor of Joseph T. Lienhard, S.J.*, edited by Ronnie J. Rombs and Alexander Y. Hwang, 68–85. Washington, DC: The Catholic University of America Press, 2010.

Jackson, B. Darrell. "Sources of Origen's Doctrine of Freedom." *Church History* 35 (1966) 13–23. Reprinted in *Doctrines of Human Nature, Sin, and Salvation in the Early Church*, edited by Everett Ferguson, 1–11. Studies in Early Christianity 10. New York: Garland, 1993.

Jovanovič, Zdravko. "St. Irenaeus, *Regula Fidei* and the Ecclesiological Context of Interpretation." *Philotheos* 13 (2013) 134–40.

Kattenbusch, Ferdinand. *Das Apostolische Symbol: seine Entstehung, sein geschichtlicher Sinn, seine ursprüngliche Stellung im Kultus und in der Theologie der Kirche.* 2 vols. Leipzig: Hinrichs, 1894, 1900.

Kunze, Johannes. *Glaubensregel, Heilige Schrift und Taufbekenntnis: Untersuchungen über die dogmatische Autorität, ihr Werden und ihre Geschichte, vornehmlich in der alten Kirche.* Leipzig: Dörffling & Franke, 1899.

Lanne, Emmanuel. "'La Règle de la Vérité': Aux sources d'une expression de saint Irénée." In *Lex Orandi Lex Credendi: Miscellanea in onore di P. Cipriano Vagaggini*, edited by G. J. Békés and G. Fernedi, 57–70. Studia Anselmiana 79. Rome: Anselmiana, 1980.

Litfin, Bryan M. "The Rule of Faith in Augustine." *Pro Ecclesia* 14 (2005) 85–101.

———. "Tertullian's Use of the *Regula Fidei* as an Interpretive Device in *Adversus Marcionem*." *Studia Patristica* 42 (2006) 405–10.

Lührmann, Dieter. "Gal 2:9 und die katholischen Briefe: Bemerkungen zum Kanon und zur *regula fidei*." *Zeitschrift für die neuentestamentliche Wissenschaft* 73 (1981) 65–87.

Ohme, Heinz. *Kanon Ekklesiastikos: Die Bedeutung des altkirchlichen Kanonbegriffs.* Berlin: de Gruyter, 1998.

Bibliography

Osborn, Eric. "Reason and the Rule of Faith in the Second Century AD." In *The Making of Orthodoxy*, edited by Rowan Williams, 40–61. Cambridge: Cambridge University Press, 1989.

Oulton, J. E. L. and H. Chadwick. *Alexandrian Christianity*. Library of Christian Classics, Vol. II. Philadelphia: Westminster, 1954.

Outler, Albert C. "Origen and the *Regulae Fidei*." *Church History* 8 (1939) 212–21. Reprinted in *The Second Century* 4 (1984) 133–41.

Paice, R. J. R. "Irenaeus on the Authority of Scripture, the Rule of Truth, and Episcopacy." Two Parts. *Churchman* 117 (2003) 57–70, 133–52.

Patterson, W. P. *The Rule of Faith*. London: Hodder & Stoughton, 1912.

Patteruparampil, Jobi. "*Regula Fidei* in Ephrem's *Hymni de Fide* LXVII and in *Sermones de Fide* IV." *Studia Patristica* 64 (2013) 177–97.

Quasten, Johannes. "Regula fidei." In *Lexikon für Theologie und Kirche*, vol. 8, edited by Josef Höfer and Karl Rahner, 1103. Freiburg: Herder, 1961.

Radner, Ephraim, and George Sumner, eds. *The Rule of Faith: Scripture, Canon, and Creed in a Critical Age*. Harrisburg, PA: Morehouse, 1998.

Smith, Joseph P., trans. *St. Irenaeus Proof of the Apostolic Preaching*. Ancient Christian Writers 16. Westminster, MD: Newman, 1952.

Smulders, Pieter. "Some Riddles in the Apostles` Creed, II. Creeds and Rules of Faith." *Bijdragen tijdschrift voor filosofie en theologie* (1971) 350–66.

Stewart, Alistair. "'The Rule of Faith . . . which He Received Through Baptism' (*Haer* 1.9.4): Catechesis, Ritual, and Exegesis in Irenaeus's Gaul." In *Irenaeus: Life, Scripture, Legacy*, edited by Sara Parvis and Paul Foster, 151–58. Minneapolis: Fortress, 2012.

Turck, André. *Évangelisaton et catéchèse aux deux premiers siècles*. Parole et mission 3. Paris: Cerf, 1962.

Van den Eynde, Damien. *Les Normes de l'Enseignement Chrétien dans la littérature patristique des trois premiers siècles*. Paris: Gembloux, J. Ducolot, 1933.

Westra, L. H. "*Regula Fidei* and Other Creedal Formulations in the *Acts of Peter*." In *The Apocryphal Acts of Peter: Magic, Miracles and Gnosticism*, edited by J. N. Bremmer, 134–47. Leuven: Peeters, 1998.

Young, Frances M. *The Making of the Creeds*. London: SCM, 1991.

Zahn, Theodor. "Glaubensregel." In *Realencyklopädie für protestantische Theologie und Kirche*, edited by Albert Hauck, 684–85. Leipzig: Hinrichs, 1899.

———. "Glaubensregel und Taufbekenntnis in der alten Kirche." *Zeitschrift für kirchliche Wissenschaft und kirchliche Leben* 2 (1881) 302–24.

Index of Scriptures

OLD TESTAMENT

Genesis   31, 79

Numbers

16   24

Psalms   79–80

30   31
36:1   25
45:7–8   37
64:5–6   26

Joel

3:2   14

NEW TESTAMENT 32

Matthew

22:34—27:63   26, 77
22:36–40   88
24:4–5   29
24:20–28   74
24:26   75

28:19   39

John

1:1–5   18
1:1–3   7
1:3   11
16:7   7
20:22   78

Acts   35

2:4   78
8:37   63

Romans

10:9   85
12:3   25

1 Corinthians

7:1–4   26
8:6   39
13:2   27
15:1–9   88
15:3–5   35
15:3–4   7
15:42–43   12

15:44   26n11

Galatians
2:9   55n17
2:14   21, 55
6:16   21, 23,
                            55

Ephesians
1:10   38
3:18–19   78
6:21   26

Philippians
2:10–11   4

Titus
2:1   25

Jude
3   2

Revelation
11:1   46

Index of Ancient Writers and Writings

Acts of Justin Martyr   35
5–7   70
2, recension B   3

Acts of Peter   59

Ambrose of Milan
Commentary on Luke   78

Apostolic Constitutions   10
7.41.3   63

Athanasius of Alexandria
Against the Arians
3.27, 28, 35, 58   61

Augustine of Hippo   29–32,
33, 58,
61–62,
79–81

Against Julian
1.6   31
2.5.10   78

On Agreement among the Evangelists
1.1.2   31, 62, 80

On Baptism (Against the Donatists)
6.25.47   80

Confessions
8.12.30   30

On Christian Doctrine   78
3.2.2   77
3.5   77

City of God
11.33   62

On Eighty-Three Varied Questions
69.1   79

Enchiridion
15.56   81

On the Grace of Christ and Original Sin
2.29.34   81

On the Merits and Forgiveness of Sins
2.27.43   80

Nature and Origin of the Soul (On the Soul and Its Origin)
2.11.15   79
2.17.23   79, 80

On the One Baptism
5.7   31

Sermons
7.3   31
59.1   30
213.2   30
213.12   81
215.2   31
265.9   78
362.7   80

On the Symbol (or *Creed*)
1.1   31

The Trinity
2.1.2   31
2.10.7   62, 80
8.6.9   31

True Religion
7.12   32

On the Literal Interpretation of Genesis
1   31, 79

12.14   80

Exposition on (Explanation of) the Psalms
4.21.8 (on Ps 30)   31
9.6   79–80
74.12   79
100.7   31
                           Letter
108.6   31
147.14.34   78
187.29   80
193.4.11   80

Tractates on John (Exposition of the Gospel of John)
98.7   78
105.8   78

Basil of Caesarea
On the Holy Spirit
27   57–58

Clement of Alexandria
                          19–21,
                          33, 53,
                          55, 57,
                              64
Miscellanies
1.1.15.2   21, 69
1.19.96   20
3.9.66   21
3.12.79.4   19
3.18.105.1   19
4.1.3.2   19
4.15.98   19
5.1.1.4   21, 77
6.15.123   21
6.15.124.5   20, 77

6.15.125.3	20, 77
6.15.127	21
6.18.165	20
7.3.13.4	19
7.7.41	20
7.15.90.5	20, 21, 78
7.16.94.5	19
7.16.95	74
7.16.105	19
7.16.105.5	20

Clement of Rome
First Clement

1:3	16
7:2	16
41:1	16
46.6	39

Didascalia Apostolorum
(***Teaching of the Apostles***)
10, 45–46

Dionysius of Corinth
16–17, 33

Ephrem the Syrian	64–65

Hymns on Faith

13.5	65

Sermons on Faith

IV,45	65

Eusebius	65

Church History

4.23.4	17
5.24.6	17
5.28.13	17
6.13.3	21
7.30.6	74

Hippolytus of Rome	8–9, 33

Against Noetus (*Contra haeresin Noeti*)   44–45, 74

1	8
14	45
17–18	8–9

Irenaeus of Lyon   3–6, 17–19, 33, 35–40, 50, 51–52, 53, 55, 58–60

Against Heresies (*Adversus Haereses*)   3, 72

1.1–8	72
1.1–8, 11–21	35n3
1.3.6	37
1.9.4—1.10.2	72
1.9.4—1.10.1	39
1.9.4	56, 63, 70, 77
1.9.5	3, 68
1.10.1	4, 35, 62
1.10.4	71
1.22.1	18
2.27	60
2.27.1	18, 76
2.28.1	17–18
2.30.9	18
3	51
3.1.2	37
3.4.2	5, 37
3.11.1	18, 37
3.11.3	37
3.12.6	18
3.15.1	18
3.16.6	38
4.6.5	38
4.33.7	5, 36
4.35.4	18, 76
5.20.1	36–37, 69

Index of Ancient Writers and Writings

Demonstration of the Apostolic Preaching   3, 36, 46
1   72
6   6, 19, 36, 71
6–7   39
8–42a   71
42b-97   71
47   37
98   18, 69, 71

John Cassian   62

John Chrysostom
Catechetical Homilies
2.20–21   63

Justin Martyr   3
Dialogue with Trypho   46
85.2   70

2 Apology
6   70

Lucian of Samosata
On the Death of Peregrinus
11–16   69

Martyrdom of Apollonius
8; 15; 36–37   70

Melito of Sardis
On the Pascha   69

Novatian   13–14, 29, 33, 46

On the Trinity
1   13
11, 17, 21   29
29   14

On Jewish Foods
7   29

Origen   10–13, 24–29, 33, 41–44, 52–53, 57, 61, 65, 85–86

Against Celsus
1.7   28
3.55   70
5.18–19   26

Dialogue with Heraclides
p437–8   28
10   26

On First Principles (De principiis)   10–13, 41–43
preface 3–8   11–13, 24, 85–86
preface 3   69
1.5.4   25
1.6.1   24
1.7.1   24
3.1.1   24
3.1.7   25
3.2.4   24
3.3.4   25, 76
3.5.3   25

4.2.2	25	4.3.3	25
4.2.7	27	5.1.27	25
4.3.14	25	10.6	25

Homilies on Leviticus
5.10.3 — 28

Commentary on 1 Corinthians
on 7:1–4 — 26

Homilies on Numbers
9.1 — 24–25

Commentary on Ephesians
fragment 36 — 26

Homilies on Joshua
7.6 — 24, 25

Commentary on Titus
PG 14.1303C–1306A — 29n14

On Psalms
64:5–6 — 26

Pamphilius of Caesarea
Apology — 42

Homilies on Jeremiah
5.14.1 — 25, 76

Patrick of Ireland — 72
Confession
4 — 72

Commentary on Matthew
10.14 — 24
11.15, 17 — 24
15.7 — 24
17.29 — 26
17.35 — 24
on 22:34—27:63 — 26, 77
on 24:20–28 — 74
series 33 on 24:4–5 — 28–29
Series 46 — 24, 74–75

Philo of Alexandria — 17

Polycrates of Ephesus — 17, 33

Prosper of Aquitaine — 62

Pseudo-Hippolytus
Theophany — 63

Homilies on Luke
25.6 — 25

Rufinus — 11–13, 25, 52

Commentary on John
13.16.98 — 25
32.187–93 — 27

Tertullian of Carthage — 6–8, 21–24, 30, 33, 40–41, 50, 53, 57, 64

Commentary on Romans
2.7.3 — 25

Index of Ancient Writers and Writings

Against Hermogenes

1	23
17	22

Against Marcion   40, 55, 60, 75

1.1.5	23
1.9	21
1.20.1	23
1.21.4	22
3.2.1	22
3.17	61
3.17.5	22, 76
4.2	23
5.8	22
5.19	21–22
5.20	22, 23

Against Praxeas   73–74

2	7–8, 40–41, 73
3.1	23
20.3	23

Apology

46.18	24
47.10	23

On Fasting

1	23

On the Flesh of Christ

6	22

On Modesty

19.3	24

On Monogamy

2.3	24

On the Prescription of Heretics (Prescription against Heretics)

Preamble	73
9	60
12.5	23, 77
13	6–7, 40–41, 73
13.1, 6	23
14	24
19	61
20.9	22–23
21	69
26.9	24
27.1	69
37.1	23
42.7	22

On Shows

4	41

On the Soul

1.6	22
2.7	23

On the Veiling of Virgins   73

1	40
1.3–4	7

Victorinus of Pettau   14–15, 33, 72

Commentary on the Apocalypse

11	72
11.1	15, 46

Vincent of Lérins   58, 62

Printed in Great Britain
by Amazon